P9-DCU-828

MORE
PODIUM
HUMOR

OTHER BOOKS BY JAMES C. HUMES

Instant Eloquence (1973)
Podium Humor (1975)
Roles Speakers Play (1976)
How to Get Invited to the White House (1977)
A Speaker's Treasury of Anecdotes about the Famous (1978)
Churchill, Speaker of the Century (1980)
Talk Your Way to the Top (1980)
Primary, a novel, co-author (1980)
Standing Ovation (1988)
Sir Winston Method (1991)
The Ben Franklin Factor (1992)
My Fellow Americans—Presidential Addresses that Shaped History (1992)
Citizen Shakespeare (1993)

MORE PODIUM HUMOR

USING WIT AND HUMOR IN
EVERY SPEECH YOU MAKE

JAMES C. HUMES

HarperPerennial
A Division of HarperCollinsPublishers

MORE PODIUM HUMOR. Copyright © 1993 by James C. Humes. All rights reserved. Printed in the United States of America. No part of this book may be used or reproduced in any manner whatsoever without written permission except in the case of brief quotations embodied in critical articles and reviews. For information address HarperCollins Publishers, Inc., 10 East 53rd Street, New York, NY 10022.

HarperCollins books may be purchased for educational, business or sales promotional use. For information, please write: Special Markets Department, HarperCollins Publishers, Inc., 10 East 53rd Street, New York, NY 10022.

FIRST HARPERPERENNIAL EDITION

Designed by Alma Hochhauser Orenstein

Library of Congress Cataloging-in-Publication Data
Humes, James C.
   More podium humor : using wit and humor in every speech you make /
James C. Humes. — 1st ed.
      p. cm.
   Continues author's Podium humor.
   Includes index.
   ISBN 0-06-273225-0
   1. Public speaking. 2. American wit and humor. I. Title.
PN4193.I5H79   1993
   808.5'1—dc20   92-54685

93 94 95 96 97 ❖/RRD 10 9 8 7 6 5 4 3 2

To DON WHITEHEAD,

who has always laughed loudest and longest at my stories

Contents

Acknowledgments

I WANT TO THANK all of those friends over the years who have listened to me tell stories—for the second and even the third time—Bob Butera, John LeBoutillier, Eliot Curson, Trevor Armbrister, Ray Tyrrell, Bill Schulz, Charles Reilly, and Granville Toogood.

Another appreciated group of dining companions is the Double-Six/Windy Corner of the Union League in Philadelphia. Some of them include Rod Ross, Perrin Hamilton, Clayton Thomas, Bob Miller, Dick Nourie, Joe Stevens, Howard Bacon, Bob McConnell, Victor Mauck, Frank Keenan, Dan Murphy, Austin Lee, George Higham and Marshall Schmidt. Bob Graves also contributed some of his stories.

I also want to mention Wolfgang Neumann, whose innate continental charm and manners encourages any raconteur.

Two others who make a storyteller's day are Tom O'Neill and John Del Rosso.

Particularly do I thank Ahnee Voelker who laboriously read my scribbled notes and typed up my anecdotes.

Introduction

IN THE EIGHTEEN YEARS SINCE I WROTE *Podium Humor* I have delivered almost 1800 talks, speeches, lectures, and seminars. The experience only confirmed the impressions I gained while searching through libraries for material for *More Podium Humor*.

I pored through fat tomes of joke anthologies and found mostly chaff and a few golden kernels of wheat. Most of the jokes were in the early post-war mode: women drivers, mothers-in-law, lecherous salesmen, and stupid spendthrift housewives. I thought that if I was embarrassed to tell these stories in a luncheon address, my readers would be embarrassed as well.

I found that no joke collection tailored the stories to fit a point, e.g., urgency, importance of communication, controversial nature, complexity of a problem, etc.

That was my intention in *Podium Humor* and its success is not only proven by its sales figures but also an unsolicited letter from a college president.

Dr. Theodore Friend, President of Swarthmore College, wrote, "Unlike any other speech book I have run across you have offered material that I can use without risking groans from the audience. It is an intelligent man's guide to humor."

Actually, I had hoped in 1972 for a larger book. My thinking was that big anthologies of humor sell better than slimmer books. The buyer in the store thinks to himself that in such a 1000-page volume there must be a couple of good stories. However, after wading through the book he usually finds that he has wasted his money.

My book was smaller because of the limitations of my own selection process. First, I must have already heard the anecdote delivered to an audience effectively; secondly, it must be an anecdote that I would use myself. I applied these criteria to *More Podium Humor*.

I have the experience of speaking in all fifty states, from Key West, Florida, to Fairbanks, Alaska, and in 26 countries from Crete to South Korea and from Argentina to China.

One lesson I learned is that you don't necessarily have to trigger guffaws to entertain an audience while making your point. That is why so much of my humor is drawn from biographies that I have read. Anecdotes about Lincoln, Churchill or Lyndon Johnson work better than contrived jokes about traveling salesmen. Because the audience can picture Churchill, the point of a story etches a deeper and more lasting impression. Anecdotes are more believable and so they are better. They entertain the audience without embarrassing the speaker.

Some of my readers have written to say they keep *Podium Humor* in the bathroom or by the bedside to open at random and enjoy a silent laugh. I appreciate their letters but my main purpose remains the same: to write for the would-be-speaker who is looking for that humorous story to emphasize a point and enliven a presentation.

James Humes
Philadelphia

PART I

The Anatomy of Humor

I

A Speaker's Strategy

WHEN YOU'VE SPOKEN IN ALL 50 STATES—not to mention 26 countries—you learn something about speaking and the use of humor in speaking. Sure, my experience in writing for all the Republicans who have served in the White House since Eisenhower helped—but the big advantage in being a former White House speechwriter is the prestige factor, which helps win speech invitations. But just to be able to deliver a talk is not enough for someone whose competition on the speech circuit is a galaxy of celebrities who only have to be seen in person by their audience to command their high fees.

I am not a household name. Yet I make close to six figures on speaking fees. I do that by so wowing the audiences that the word-of-mouth reaction to my talks leads to further invitations. My secret is simple: preparation. I address audiences *naked*—that is, without a lectern in front of me. (If I need a microphone, it is a *lavaliere* or lapel mike). The cost of speaking without notes is hard work—it means writing out a talk and committing it to memory beforehand—but it pays off in face-to-face audience eye contact. As I said, the secret of my success is preparation, but the secret inside the secret is *stories*—hilarious, uplifting, entertaining anecdotes taken from my own life or, most often, from the pages of books about the great and famous.

The more stories you have in your talk, the less you have to memorize word-for-word. Think about it. When you tell an audience the crazy, weird and funny things that happened to you—the college prank, the tyrannical sergeant in basic training, the hotel mix-up in your honeymoon or the time the slides were reversed in your corporate presentation— you don't have to write out what happened. You just say it as you have scores of times, probably polishing if not embellishing it in the process.

At the speech course I teach at the University of Pennsylvania, I ask my graduate students to give me their IRA's as their first assignment. IRA's, or Incident Recorded Accounts, have a forensic, not a financial, purpose. I make students write down the funny, crazy and poignant stories they often tell about their lives.

And then I point out to my students how each story can illustrate a point in a talk. Perhaps the hotel foul-up was due to a lack of planning. The tyrannical sergeant was one who lacked the necessary skills in communication. The slide disaster was caused by a failure to attend to details. All of these are potential points in an executive talk.

Personal experiences are also great for you, the speaker. When you talk about something that happened to you, you come alive and give your talk energy and excitement. You also enthrall your audience. Personal experiences deliver personality power. The more you give of yourself to the audience the more they will like you. And the more they like you the more they will respond to your message.

So the first job for the would-be speaker is to jot down all the comic mishaps, misadventures and mistakes you sometimes tell friends about. Then, turn them over in your mind and figure how they can be told to push a point: a need for action, better planning, cutting excessive costs, clarifying poor messages, improving little support, enhancing marketing efforts, etc.

LECTURE BUSINESS

America is a nation of clubs. Clubs have to have programs and programs require speakers. A French count came to America in the early part of the last century and reported back that the new democracy seemed to be run by all sorts of societies, organizations and clubs in communities and towns.

Count Alexis de Tocqueville was right and that's why America is the only country in the world to have lecture bureaus.

It was the demand for speakers by women's clubs that first triggered the rise of the lecture bureau. The first speakers represented by bureaus were Oscar Wilde, Mark Twain and young Winston Churchill, fresh from his Boer War experience. Today, lecture bureaus are still conduits for celebrities. A lecture bureau will locate for the Podunk Chamber of Commerce a famous personality and deliver him for a fat fee, from which the bureau takes its 25 percent or more cut.

If you are not famous, you must have at least a connection with fame to be sought out by a lecture agent. Mine was being a White House speechwriter and I have been represented by bureaus for over twenty years. But fame is fleeting and the fact that I once wrote for yesterday's presidents is no longer enough of a cachet to excite lecture bureaus. My speaking engagements these days come through repeat invitations from organizations that booked me in the past.

My formula for speechwriting was what I call the Michener Method: James Michener has written best sellers about

Africa, Alaska, Hawaii and Texas. Each novel is filled with enough romance and adventure to keep you turning the pages—but at the end you also take away the satisfaction of having learned something about the history of a land and its people.

This is similar to a speaker's desire to enlighten an audience as he entertains them. The speaker has to keep the audience's attention as he talks but at the end he wants his audience to feel that they have learned something useful. The speaker has a certain expertise and experience he or she can share with the audience but he must do it in an entertaining fashion. This does not mean a series of jokes. If you resort to that, you might entertain an audience temporarily but in the end give them nothing solid to take away with them. It's like substituting a chocolate sundae for a full course appetizing dinner. Sure, you enjoyed the confectionery concoction, but you get little content for the calories.

Ronald Reagan was a has-been actor who talked his way first into the governorship of Calfornia and then the presidency of the United States. He perfected his ability to persuade—not as an actor but as a speaker.

In the sixties he spoke for General Electric four times a week, sometimes three times a day. It was generally the same talk in which he told the same stories. The more he recounted his anecdotes the more he refined his delivery and tuning to perfection. That's why stories you often tell friends are sure-fire material. You don't have to read from a script, because a story that tickles your fancy or funny bone will stay with you, particularly as you tell it a few times to your family and friends.

As an entertainer, Reagan at first prepared his talks by thinking of all the stories he could use to illustrate a theme, such as the danger of big government, and then organizing a talk around the stories. Most speakers do the reverse. They write out their talk and then try to find stories to fit the point they want to make.

Take a cue from "the Great Communicator": list some of the funny things that have happened to you and then see how you can shape and adapt them for the purpose of your talk. Then add to your own personal file some of the funny stories or anecdotes from the collection in this book. If you are in business, look at the *Executive Suite* chapter, but don't forget to also check the index for the topics you plan to go over, e.g., costs, planning, sales, marketing, profit, etc.

HUMOR—NOT JOKES

Humor is not just a weapon to be wielded at the beginning of the talk. Too many speakers think that the only time to tell a funny story is to break the ice at the beginning of the talk. I regularly have calls from CEO's who say "Jamie, give me a funny story to open with. I need something to break the ice." I tell them "Look, there's no eleventh commandment that says you have to begin with a funny story. Anyway that's the hardest time to get a laugh because the audience is expecting it." It is true that a funny story will trigger a bigger chuckle if placed in the middle of your talk, when the audience is not expecting humor, than at the beginning, when they are. As Aristotle once said, "Humor is the familiar at the unexpected moment."

Former President Ford said in *People* magazine that "James Humes provided the raisins in the muffin." In other words, in the anecdotes I provided, I put raisins all through the muffin, not just one on top. Humorous stories throughout the speech are more than ice breakers, they are mind wakers. They refreshen interest, score a point and tickle the mind.

Mind-Wakers—which are anecdotes told throughout

your talk—don't have to be riotously funny. As long as they illustrate a point or exemplify a problem, they serve their purpose. When you telegraph a joke in the very beginning by saying "That reminds me of a story . . . " you raise the anticipation of the audience and put too much of a burden on the story and your delivery skills. The result invites an anti-climax—a forced laugh from an audience that makes a speaker look more foolish than funny.

By all means, if you have to open with a funny story, feel free to pick one of my anecdotes, but don't stop there. Keep the audience entertained by spicing up your talk with two or three more.

You will note that I don't refer to humorous stories as jokes. A joke is to humor what pornography is to erotica. An obscene picture out of context is pornographic, but a love scene that unfolds between two well-developed characters in a novel is exciting. A joke is something tacked onto a talk. Humor is wit interwoven into your talk. A joke is a story that serves no purpose except to garner a cheap laugh; a joke becomes a humorous story when it illustrates a serious point in an entertaining way.

This book is not titled *More Podium Jokes*—it is *More Podium Humor*—stories to be told by speakers from the podium or the dais. Sure, you can read this book for fun and amusement, but I want you to be checking each story out as potential for your next podium appearance. Think of the stories as forensic fodder or as your own warehouse of wit for winning over audiences.

2

Confessions of a
White House Ghost

I.R.A.'s

WE HAVE ALL HAD SOME crazy experiences in our work or in
our lives. Write some of them down as your I.R.A. (Incident
Recorded Account) and build up your inventory of stories.
You don't have to write out the whole story, just a phrase to
entitle it—such as *Shoe Story* (you had to make an early
morning presentation and when you arrived at the city you
realized you had on one brown shoe and one black shoe).
And then add words that further define the experience, like
planning and *preparation*.

In this same way I have written down some of the stories
I use in talks. One of these is *Ike—Rest Room—Planning*.

In 1956 I was a Young Republican volunteer assigned as
Sergeant-at-Arms to a $1000 a plate dinner in Washington
when President Eisenhower was the featured speaker. Just
before Ike was due to appear on the dais one of his detail
spotted me and asked where the men's room was. The President, who had just recovered from intestinal surgery, was
suffering some discomfort below his belt.

Now I didn't know whether the men's room in this football field–size arena was all the way around on the left or right, but not wanting to look stupid, I pointed and said "Right" and then started to run down the corridor to make sure. To my dismay, I found it was the ladies room. I looked around and saw the President rounding the corner far away. So I yelled. "Everybody out, everybody out—Emergency— President of the United States." Two ladies immediately scrambled out looking like flushed grouse. I pulled the door frontwards and pushed it back to the wall to hide the telltale sign. And then with my hand in salute, the President entered the ladies' room. He must have noticed that the accoutrements didn't belong to the male gender, for when he exited, his blue eyes drilled two holes in me. The old general had expected better staff planning!

Two other Ike stories—while not necessarily hilarious— are still entertaining insights. One time, Ike mentioned to a group of us that General Douglas MacArthur had an "eye" problem. Immediately I thought that MacArthur must have suffered from glaucoma or a detached retina, but then Ike added, Yes, Mac had an addiction to the perpendicular pronoun—"I." The message from this story is to keep the ego under control.

That is a great point to make to fellow executives. Eisenhower again displayed such ego discipline in the next story. After Eisenhower retired to Gettysburg from the White House, the old general was visited by another general. The talk turned to Vietnam and Ike's visitor said of the press: "Herodotus, in his work on the Peloponnesian Wars wrote, 'You can't be an armchair general 28 miles from the front.'"

Later, after the former president's visitor left, I asked about that quotation, for at the time I had a hobby of collecting quotations and I wanted to get this one exactly right. Eisenhower answered, "First, it was not Herodotus—it was

Aemilius Paulus—secondly, it wasn't the Peloponnesian Wars with Persia—it was the Punic Wars with Carthage, and third he misquoted."

When I asked why he didn't say anything, General Eisenhower answered: "You don't understand, I got where I did by hiding my ego."

Well, I didn't hide my ego when I was asked to write the plaque to be left on the moon when the Apollo mission landed on it in the summer of 1969. First, I penned "Here men from the planet earth first set upon the moon in July 1969. We came in peace for all mankind." Afterwards, on a lark, I offered this for the plaque: "Just As Man Explores Space, Hope Unites Mankind Exalting Science."

It was an acronym that spells my name. Of course, it was turned down but I use the story to introduce an acronym in a speech-organizing formula for short talks: E.A.S.E., which stands for Exemplify, Amplify, Specify, Electrify.

THE SPIRIT OF THE OCCASION

In dealing with the competition, sometimes you have to turn the competitor's marketing or strategy to your own advantage.

In 1962, I was running for the Pennsylvania legislative against an entrenched incumbent. He attacked me for being a carpet-bagger and not owning property. It was true that I had just moved back to the city and was only renting an apartment.

At the talk I said that I didn't think it mattered whether you first came in to the district with your clothes on or off. But after stating my education platform, I said, "Actually, I am a native. I was born in Williamsport but my opponent was not. (He had moved there in his 20's to practice as a dentist.) Then I said that it shouldn't matter whether you owned property or not—and I gave my economic platform. Then I added as a closer, "Actually, I really do own property" and I pulled out from my jacket a huge paper which I unfolded before an expectant audience. "Here is the deed to Wildwood Cemetery, where four generations now rest and so God willing will a fifth."

The emotional ending resulted in an endorsement.

The topic of ancestry prompts me to tell another anecdote which I use to impose the need for 'spirit.'

When I met the Duke of Edinburgh as an exchange student in Britain at age 18, I wore a Scottish plaid tie. I didn't know that most English make fun of Americans for flaunting their Scottish ties.

Prince Philip asked, "Why do all you Americans like to proclaim your Scotch background?" I replied, "My mother, who was a schoolteacher, always told me that Scotch was a liquid, but Scottish the adjective."

Prince Phillip replied, "Young man, you may be correct but I venture to say that more 'Scotch' flows in American veins than Scottish!" The Prince's bon mot is a lead-in to call for an organization or occasion's need for the right 'spirit.'

In my speech communications seminars, I tell the following anecdote to stress that the ear is one-tenth the receptive organ that the eye is; that is, we record visual images more easily than spoken words. That is why an article read out loud cannot be used as a talk. In 1982, I was in Newport, Rhode Island, to deliver a speech seminar at the Naval War College. When I came down for breakfast, an elegant gentleman in an ascot and Norfolk tweed jacket called out.

"James Humes, isn't it? Will you join me for breakfast?"

I recognized his face immediately but I couldn't think of his name. But as a one-time politician who had served in the state legislature I bluffed it. "Well, how the heck are you— you're looking more distinguished than ever."

He answered "James, do you remember when we met in the Ritz Hotel in London—you were just writing a book on Churchill?"

"Of course," I said. "Actually that book has gone into paperback."

After the second cup of coffee, I had run out of small talk and tried the old conversational gambit. "Tell me, how's the family?"

The words had no sooner left my mouth than I recognized who that breakfast companion with the astonished look on his face was: Claus von Bülow. The playboy socialite at that time was facing the charge of attempted murder of his wife—the action having been brought by his wife's children.

That wins the "red-face" of the year award—and I tell it to show that we remember many more faces than the names that go with those faces because the eye records better. A talk—unlike an article—should be shaped to be heard by the ear, not read by the eye.

Another embarrassing moment I use in talks was an occasion I arrived late in Madison, Wisconsin, just as dessert was being served. I launched into my scheduled talk on Churchill without even having time to look at the program.

I spoke of Churchill as a master of language and I related some of the expressions he had coined for the English language: 'iron curtain' and 'summit conference.' Then I told how Churchill made as a synonym for traitor the name of Vidkun Quisling, the Norwegian collaborator with the Nazis. I imitated Churchill spitting out the words. "These vile quislings within our midst." The way Churchill hissed out the word quisling, I told the audience, suggested something serpentine that had slithered out from under a rock.

My talk was greeted with deafening silence. It was followed by a presentation of the Silver Medal of Service, which was to be awarded to a distinguished doctor of the community, Dr. Norge Quisling. He was, in fact, a cousin of the executed Nazi.

Sometimes, however, you can oversell your audience. That is the point I make by telling another embarrassing experience. In a talk in Omaha in 1984, I closed "My Evening with Churchill" with a poignant account of the ninety-year-old dying Churchill holding hands, without speaking, with his old comrade in arms, General Eisenhower, in 1964. I followed that with another 'wet handkerchief' story of Eisenhower at Churchill's funeral, where the kings and President de Gaulle all sang, pursuant to Churchill's will instructions, the "Battle Hymn of the Republic." The third verse goes "He sounded out the trumpet that never called retreat. His will goes marching on."

The emotional ending triggered a standing ovation, except for one aged lady in the front row who did not stand. She had died during the talk. It was a macabre example of "slaying your audience."

LIFE'S MOST EMBARRASSING MOMENTS

Royalty prompts this anecdote, which I apply to the theme of purpose or objective, specifically, not letting yourself stray from the task at hand.

In December 1952, I was visiting a school friend whose father, a retired Brigadier, was the Steward or Manager of Sandringham, a royal castle. My fortuitous presence won me an invitation to a private 16th birthday celebration that the Queen was having for her cousin, Princess Alexandra. At the small dance, an equerry indicated that it was appropriate for me to dance with Her Majesty. The Queen was at the time 26—with three striking things about her appearance: her short stature (5'1"), her rosy fair English complexion and an impressive cleavage. My 6'2" height gave me an advantageous view down her low-cut gown. Yet, thinking I could be carried off to the Tower of London for such an act of *lèse-majesté*, I stared resolutely at the ceiling as I danced, responding monosyllabically to the Queen's polite conversational questions—"Did I like an English Christmas? Do I miss my family?" Keeping my eyes trained upward on the rococo pattern in the ceiling, I treaded on the royal toes.

The previous story is an example of what I call a Negative Name Drop. It means impressing your audience with a famous name but softening the bluster of braggadocio by putting yourself down at the same time. Think back to any occasion when your path was tangled with the great or famous. If you handled yourself stupidly or clumsily, the experience could be a potential anecdote. Your connection with celebrities makes you more interesting as a speaker, yet your ineptness on the occasion endears you to your listeners. The combination of awe and affection makes you a winning personality.

A negative name-dropping story I tell to illustrate the need to communicate clearly is the time I drafted a speech for Ronald Reagan. Former Governor Reagan came to Philadelphia in 1975 to deliver a speech to the World Affairs Council. His speech was an endeavor to trumpet his foreign policy credentials and he spoke on the situation in Asia and Africa. In the speech I wrote, the phrase *third world* was used seven times. At the hotel in Philadelphia where Reagan delivered his address, I sat at a table which included Senator Schweiker and Walter Annenberg, former Ambassador to Great Britain. All knew I had helped draft Reagan's address. Unfortunately, when Reagan spoke he added the word *war* to "third world"—"third world *war*"—as in "We must address ourselves to the problem of the "third world war."

Reagan did this not once, but seven times. Each time my

eminent audience looked at me and I wanted to hide under the table.

The garbled phrase by the Great Communicator Ronald Reagan recalls an incident when my own words were misconstrued. As a Director of Policy and Plans in the U.S. Department of State, I was asked to deliver an address to an international audience in Washington. The topic was foreign aid and I tried to put across the idea that other things besides economic well-being, such as legal institutions, a representative government and other free institutions, were more important to the stability of a nation. My secretary typed up my remarks and I reviewed them. Then, as an afterthought, I dictated a title for my speech inspired by the Bible. It was "Man shall not live on bread alone." My secretary, who was shortly to be wed, must have had other things on her mind when she heard my words. The next week, when I spoke, the program announcing my address had the title of my talk emblazoned on it as "Man shall not love in bed alone." This experience is one I relate to stress the importance of teamwork or group planning.

That was not the only time I suffered a red face from a failure in translation. At the University of Osaka, where I was to speak on the American presidency, a Japanese professor seated to my right rose and spoke for fifteen minutes in Japanese. At the end I joined in the enthusiastic applause. A little later the Japanese translator whispered to me that I had been clapping at my own introduction. I sometimes tell that story to congratulate a group effort in which I took part.

We all have embarrassing moments in life that can entertain audiences. I remember one time when I was not exactly embarrassed, but was, to say the least, nonplused.

I had ridden from Port Moresby, the capital of Papua New Guinea, to a little village in the equatorial islands. I took along my jacket, but did not wear it. When I arrived, I was greeted by the mayor. He was more formally dressed with a top hat and morning coat—the kind you see rented for weddings. Except there was nothing below the waist, not even a loin cloth.

Yet his elegant upper attire demanded some adaptation on my part. So I put on my coat to receive his welcome.

Think back to all the "life's most embarrassing moments" in your life. List them, caption them and give them a point. Make them part of your podium humor.

3

Rules of a Raconteur

A GOOD STORYTELLER has to know two things: what story to tell and how to tell it.

THE THREE R's

There are three R's in the choice of story: Relevance, Realism and Retellability. What turns a joke into humor is the relevance of the story to your speech. If the story doesn't tell a message, don't tack it on to your talk.

Here is a story I heard from the historian Sir Arthur Bryant at the London Guildhall Banquet for the Carmen in 1963. The Carmen are a guild of people who have traced their ancestry back to carriage makers. Today, it is an association to which leading executives of the car industry belong.

Balliot College in Oxford, which I attended, offered a scholarship to a young man who not only had the potential of being a bright scholar, but also displayed moral rectitude.

The old dean who interviewed applicants was generally disapproving of the ways of the young generation. So he devised a test of word association to ferret out the morally unsuitable.

To one young man who seemed particularly smooth and glib he asked:

"Gordon, Gordon. What do you think of when you hear that name?" asked the dean, hoping the young man would say something that rhymes with sin and goes with tonic.

"General Gordon," answered the young man, "the hero of Africa, the martyr of Khartoum."

The dean nodded and posed another question. "Haig, Haig (a popular brand of scotch), "What do you think of?" expecting the lad to answer something that comes from Scotland and goes with soda.

"General Haig," was the response "The greatest general of World War I."

The old dean was still suspicious so he offered his final question.

"Vat 69, Vat 69. What do you think of?"

The young man pondered for some time and answered, "Vat 69—isn't that the Pope's telephone number?"

Gentlemen, when I hear the name Carmen I can tell you, I think of Rolls-Royce, Jaguar, Bentley, Austin, Morris and all the other names that tell the world of British auto craftsmanship.

Or here is one I told to a Republican audience in 1980 when I was taking a shot at former President Carter.

The mess we find ourselves in did not come about by accident. It took planning. It is like the idea a sultan of a Middle East emirate had back before the turn of the century. He wanted to put the newly arriving British minister in his place. So he had a tunnel installed in the anteroom next to the throne chamber to ensure that the British envoy would arrive at the sultan's throne on his knees. When the British diplomat arrived at the Palace to present his credentials, he took one look at the waist-high tunnel, and, instead of going in forward on his knees, did it the reverse way. The sultan on his throne saw emerging from the tunnel not a lowered head, but another part of the anatomy. It was not the first time a head of state got things ass-backwards!

A story punch line with a point entertains as it educates. That is the message of this book—the only humor book that offers a treasury of stories specifically tailored to hit the hundreds of points an executive is likely to make in a talk.

As you thumb through the pages of stories, you might note that I lean heavily on anecdotes about famous people and have very few that feature talking dogs or other fanciful situations.

The reason for this is Realism—the second of my Three R's. A few years ago, at the Waldorf Astoria, I heard a Nobel Prize–winning doctor at a black-tie benefit begin his talk with some joke about what a duck said to the Pope on a golf course.

Why would such an eminent man risk debasing his prestige by repeating some stupid joke he had heard?

Anecdotes about the great ring true even if some of them may be apocryphal. Other stories should be told as if they happened to you or to people you are acquainted with.

Someone once said that the best raconteurs are both actors and liars with good memories. Well, my book can substitute for your memory, but you have to tell stories as if they really happened. When you start off a story in a talk with "There was this traveling salesman . . ." everyone in the audience knows a joke is coming, but if you start off "A sales agent in a company I work with . . . " your hopes for laughter are greater because the audience is expecting a business experience, not a humorous anecdote. The surprise punch line then jolts them into laughter. Perhaps the audience will realize later that the story really didn't take place, but remember the humor as well as the poetic license.

Elton Trueblood in his book *The Wit and Humor of Christ* says that Jesus Christ was a storyteller. He made up the stories about "Good Samaritan" or "Prodigal Son" to prove a point.

For example, I tell this story about myself.

I was driving on a back road through Pennsylvania and I stopped and rolled down my window and asked a boy on a bridge with a fishing rod, "Tell me how far it is to Mill Hall?"

"Well," said the boy, "the way you are going its about 24,996 miles but if you turn around it's about four."

This is an apt story to lead in to a talk about the direction a company is going or planning to go. But imagine how flat the story is if you begin, "There was this tourist who stopped his car . . ."

Some groups will book you but then change the title of your talk. They select a title that will attract more of their members, even if it has little connection to your background. For example, once I agreed to a talk entitled "Confessions of a White House Ghost," but then I arrived at this bankers' meeting and found the following notice on the hotel bulletin board:

New York Bankers Meeting

James Humes, *Washington and the Future of Banking*

When I began speaking, I told this story.

When I was at Williams College, I took a course entitled *Survey of the New Testament.* I enrolled in this not because I had an intention towards a divine calling but because the professor was a retired Episcopalian rector, Dr. Williamson, who gave the same examination question each year: "Trace and Delineate the Travels of the Apostle Paul."

Because it was known as an easy course, we had a lot of the football players in the class. At the exam, just before Christmas, Dr. Williamson passed out the blue books and wrote on the blackboard. "Analyze and Criticize the Sermon on the Mount."

Some of the class walked out. I looked over and saw Tiny, a center on the football team, whose head was as thick as his shoulders, scribbling away.

When we came back after Christmas vacation, I saw that Tiny had gotton a B+. I asked him "Tiny, what did you write?"

"Well, Humes, when I looked at that question, 'Analyze and Criticize the Sermon on the Mount,' I wrote down 'Who am I to criticize the words of the Master—but I would like to write about the travels of the Apostle Paul.'"

So my friends, who am I to talk about banking in front of you bankers? But I would like to talk about my experience in the White House.

Actually, as you might guess, I didn't take such a course, nor did I have such an experience. But I told it as if I had.

One story I apply when I speak on controversial questions or address hostile audiences is this one:

A neighbor of mine down the block is a district sales representative for a national firm. Just after he married for the second time, he hit the top in his company's sales chart and won a week in Las Vegas at the company's regional conference.

His comely young bride did not want to attend the boring sales meetings so she took herself up to the roof sun deck to capture some decent sun. After a while she took off her top—and then later her bottoms. After all, she was all alone on the roof deck.

A little after twelve the manager came up to the deck and screamed, "Madam, you must come down."

"What's the problem—you mean planes are flying too low? I do have a towel, after all, lying over my backside."

"MADAM, DON'T YOU UNDERSTAND? YOU'RE LYING OVER THE DINING ROOM SKYLIGHT!"

And perhaps there is another side to the problem you ought to consider.

In other words, I told this story I had heard from another source as if it had happened to someone I knew. If I had started off, "There was this guy who went to Las Vegas . . . " it would have been a dud.

The story brings me to my third R: *Retellablity*. The previous story carries the spice of suggestiveness, yet it falls easily within the bounds of good taste.

X-rated stories are ones I couldn't tell my grandmother. (Yet knowing some of the grandmothers I do today, I can't imagine the kind of story that would shock them!) Generally, dirty stories are *verboten*.

Racist and sexist stories are also taboo.

Yet I've heard Jesse Jackson tell a story about his eating a watermelon. I've heard a rabbi who tells a story about Ikie, the clothes merchant. I've heard a distinguished woman executive say that she hoped she was still a sex object. In short, you *can* tell a story at the expense of yourself, your own race, your own religion or your own sex.

But how do you tell when a bawdy story crosses the line into bad taste? The line between spicy and smutty is not always clear. Let's examine at first why 'dirty' stories are a source of laughter. Is it because the sexual act is intrinsically comical? No. It's because sex has been a repressed subject ever since childhood. At the very suggestion of a sexual encounter, the air becomes filled with a note of nervous tension and then the punch line explodes the tension into laughter.

Bathroom and barnyard stories fall into the same category. The same giddy tension arises when we treat in a light way scary subjects like death or sacred subjects like Jesus, the Pope, St. Peter or Moses.

There is a talking duck story I tell in the classroom to explain the power of the taboo in the bawdy story.

The great eagle in his aerie is frustrated. He spreads his wings wide and looks down and spies a dove. He swoops down upon the dove and takes it to his aerie. Following the sounds of rustle-flustle, rustle-flustle, the contented bird floats away saying, "I'm a little dove and I just had some love."

But in a little while the great titan of the skies gets frustrated again. He spreads his wings wide and zooms upon for a lark and takes it back to his nest.

Once again we hear the sounds of rustle-flustle, rustle-flustle and the happy lark wafts away saying, "I'm a little lark and I just had some fun in the dark."

But again time passes and the mighty monarch of the mountains is frustrated again. He looks down left and right—nothing in sight. Then, way down in a little pond he sees the glimmer of a duck. He swoops down after the duck and takes the duck back to his aerie. There is a cloud of commotion—dust, twigs, feathers and then a bedraggled creature plummets from the nest saying, "I AM A LITTLE DRAKE AND THERE'S BEEN ONE AWFUL MISTAKE."

It is the expectation of the taboo four-letter word that triggers the laughter.

The German philosopher Immanuel Kant wrote, "The essence of humor is an expectation that comes to nothing."

A humorous story is like a balloon; you pump it up with details and then puncture it with a punch line. In other words: the greater the build-up, the greater the fall.

RULE OF THREE

Many stories follow the Rule of Three, a method of build-up. You have all heard stories that have three characters: the Presbyterian minister, the Catholic priest and the Jewish rabbi; or the accountant, doctor and lawyer; or the German, Frenchman or Italian; or even the first, second and third guy going into a bar or maybe even the wife summing up the attributes of her three husbands.

I tell this story to express a note of appreciation.

I overheard three businessmen sitting together on a suburban train and they each got to discussing their respective wives. The first husband said, "My wife tells me I'm so distinguished, I look like an ambassador."

The second one said, "My wife tells me I'm the best-read man she has ever met."

Then the third one added, "My wife really appreciates me. I remember one time when I had to stay home from the office, every time a mailman or delivery man arrived at the door, she shouted, 'MY HUSBAND'S HOME! MY HUSBAND'S HOME!'"

In the Rule of Three, the first two points build up the expectation and the third provides the punch line to explode it.

Another suggestive story I tell audiences is one that underscores the need to remain cool in the face of a crisis or the unexpected.

An American professor of French who wanted to find all the nuances of the phrase *savoir-faire* flew to Paris to question members of the Academie Francais.

"It's not difficult," said the first expert. "A man goes home and finds his wife with another man. What does he do? He tips his hat and says 'Bonjour, Monsieur.' He has *savoir-faire*."

But the second savant says, "That is not the precise definition of *savoir-faire*. It is when the man goes home early. He finds his wife with another man. He then tips his hat and says 'Bonjour, Monsieur, continuez (continue).' That man has *savior-faire*."

"Oh no," says the third academic, fingering his beard. "It is when the husband goes home to find his wife with another man and the husband tips his hat and says '*Bonjour, Monsieur husband, continuez*!' Now if the other man in bed can continue, *he* has *savoir-faire*."

The Three B's

What is the Rule of Three but Build-up! The first two points set up the situation for the third. Even if the Rule of Three is not used in most funny stories, the principle behind it— setting up a situation or building up a figure for a fall— Build-up is the first of the three B's for podium humor. *Build-up*, *Burst* and *Bridge*. The build-up is 'the pumping up' of a story like a balloon. The burst is the punch line that punctures that ballon and the bridge is the linking of the punch line to the point you want to make in your speech.

The next time you have to give a speech, you can flip through this collection to choose some apt stories for the occasion. If you are the kind of person who prepares a talk by putting it on paper, *never* type out the story in full.

It is hard enough to read a speech. It is impossible to read a humorous story. Instead, put down your build-up as a list of the key words, characters and situation. Follow that with the burst in block letters, underlining the trigger word.

Look at these notes:

> 18-year-old Texan G.I.
> British train
> Major, Fat lady, dog
> THEN YOU GO AND THROW OUT THE WRONG BITCH.
> Back in World War II, a young American soldier caught a crowded train to London. He entered a six-passenger train compartment where there were only five people, except that one large lady was occupying two spaces—one for her little Pekingese dog.

After half an hour the G.I. said, "Ma'am, I'm on a 48-hour pass and I would sure like to sit down."

The British woman replied, "I find you Americans very insolent."

More time passed and the private asked again. "Ma'am, I'm from Abilene, Texas, and I have my own hunting dogs back home. I wouldn't mind having that little tyke sitting on my lap, but I just *got* to sit down."

The British lady responded, "I find you Americans not only insolent but arrogant."

More time passed and the Texan said, "Ma'am I have been sitting up all night and I'm asking you for the last time—I just have to sit down."

The overstuffed British woman answered, "I find you Americans not only insolent and arrogant but downright obnoxious."

With that the G.I. opened the compartment window, picked up the Pekingese dog, threw it out the window and sat down.

A British major with clipped moustache who was observing offered a coy comment. "You Americans do everything the wrong way. In driving you drive down the wrong side of the road. In eating you pick up the fork with the wrong hand. AND THEN YOU GO AND THROW OUT THE WRONG BITCH!"

My bridge in such a story is a plug or praise for someone who does something the *right* way.

TRIGGER WORD

Once, in Pocatello, Idaho, when I had just finished telling the previous story, a bearded man interrupted me right in the middle of my talk, saying, "Mr. Humes, I am a professor of communications at the University of Idaho and you've told the story the wrong way. You should end it 'AND THEN YOU GO AND THROW THE WRONG BITCH OUT THE WINDOW.'"

I looked at him and said softly, "May I continue?"

When my speech ended to enthusiastic applause, I said, "I thank all of you but one. I have delivered hundreds of addresses but never before have I been interrupted in the middle of my talk. First, even if the professor had been correct, it would have been rude. But if I had delivered the story his way, I would have walked on the punch line. The trigger word is 'bitch' and saying 'out the window' afterwards smothers it. The trigger word in a punch line should, if at all possible, be the very last word."

The great raconteur doesn't have to know the build-up word for word; all he needs to carry with him is a picture of the general situation. When it comes to the 'burst,' however, the raconteur must etch each word into his memory.

4

Star Power

GLAMOUR IS AN APT WORD. Its original meaning is "magical charm." Famous people in history and celebrities of stage and screen have the charm of charisma.

Some years ago the publishers of *Time* magazine had a market survey done about their regular features. To their surprise the section most read and first turned to was the *People* section, which contains snappy items about what celebrities had done or said to make the news in the previous week. The popularity of the section convinced the publishers to start a new magazine called *People.*

An acquaintance of mine recently retired from advertising to run his own small town newspaper. One of the first cost-cutting steps he took was to eliminate the national gossip column by a national society writer. After all, did the people in Iowa really want to know what gown Jackie Onassis wore or whom George Hamilton was now dating or what movie role Brooke Shields hoped to land? The answer is they did—and in a few months my friend had to reinstate the society column.

We are a celebrity-driven society. The book industry is proof of that. Years ago, authors were invited to radio and T.V. talk shows on the basis of the book's contents. Now the first criterion is the author's celebrity. Why? Because stars send ratings soaring. Celebrities are besieged with invitations to appear on talk shows. And because audiences tend to buy books that they hear plugged on talk shows, book houses publish authors whose names will land them invitations to national shows.

Star power is also the reason I include so many anecdotes about the famous in this book. By their nature these stories fit the definition of the Three R's. They are real because they happened to real people. They are retellable because they can be told to any audience. And they all have a point, so you can choose one that is relevant to your talk.

But the reader asks if these anecdotes are as funny as some of the contrived comic situations story makers can concoct? Not always. Yet anecdotes about the famous—unlike jokes—carry a parachute for the storyteller. The parachute is truth and credibility. Even if the audience has only an inward chuckle, they are left with a warm insight into a famous personality.

For example, I tell the following story on an anniversary occasion, whether it be a wedding, alumni reunion or even an event honoring the founding of a company or organization some years later:

> In the early 1930's the struggling news reporter Charles MacArthur asked the emerging starlet Helen Hayes for a date in Central Park. At the moment when he asked for her hand, he pulled out a bag of peanuts and said, "Darling, I sure wish these were diamonds."
>
> Forty years later the now established playwright MacArthur again asked his famous wife to join him at a bench in Central Park.
>
> This time he pulled from his pocket another brown paper bag, emptied diamonds into Helen Hayes' hands and said,
>
> "DARLING, I SURE WISH THESE WERE PEANUTS."

On a light occasion, where among other things, I want to thank a woman for some arrangements she has made or recognize her accomplishments, I recount this anecdote about W.C. Fields.

At the Polo Lounge at the Beverly Hills Hotel, W.C. Fields took the whiskey the bartender set before him. He took a sip and said, "IT WAS WOMAN WHO DROVE ME TO DRINK [PAUSE] AND I NEVER GOT A CHANCE TO THANK HER."

Anecdotes like these can deliver laughter but they don't depend on it for their impact. And they are always entertaining! One huge advantage they have over the "guy in the bar" joke or the "golfer in the sand trap" howler is that the audience knows the celebrity. We can easily picture in our minds Helen Hayes on the park bench or W.C. Fields standing up at the bar.

From school days on I have filed away bon mots and historical encounters about the great and famous. At first, I preferred biography to fiction and I carefully gleaned memorable anecdotes for further reference.

When I was a speechwriter for former President Nixon, I offered him this anecdote concerning Benjamin Franklin as a launching pad for remarks honoring a resigning cabinet head.

In 1777, Benjamin Franklin, our Minister to France resigned to return to Philadelphia. At Versailles, Thomas Jefferson, the new Minister, was met in Versailles by Count Vergennes, the French prime minister.

Vergennes said, "Mr. Jefferson, have you come to replace Dr. Franklin?"

Jefferson replied, "NO ONE CAN EVER REPLACE BENJAMIN FRANKLIN. I AM ONLY SUCCEEDING HIM."

President Nixon liked such stories because he didn't have to memorize the whole text of prepared remarks. He could easily imprint the Jefferson–Franklin story into his memory and go on from there to cite several reasons why the particular honoree could never be replaced.

Recently, I worked with Senator Phil Gramm on his convention keynote address. He closed with this story about Abraham Lincoln.

At a critical time in the Civil War, a delegation called on President Lincoln at the White House. Lincoln told them of the time a young boy had gone with his father on a hunting trip. While asleep on the mountainside, the boy was wakened by a meteor shower. Scared, he shook his father awake.

The father said, "Son don't be concerned about the shooting stars. Keep your eyes on the fixed stars that have long been our guides."

Lincoln went on to say that if we stayed true to the ideals of our Founding Fathers, the future of the country was secure.

More than a few of the Lincoln stories in this book I fed to former Presidents Nixon and Ford in drafting White House remarks.

As readers of my other books know, my favorite hero is Winston Churchill. In Martin Gilbert's official biography of Churchill, he recounts this story:

Just before the coronation [of Queen Elizabeth II] in June 1953, Churchill had his mind on earlier Queens—Queen Elizabeth [I] and Queen Anne, whom he had written about and Queen Victoria, whom he had served. At the Commonwealth dinner on May 24, which Queen Elizabeth II attended, the 79-year-old Prime Minister was introduced to an 18-year-old American who was an English-speaking Union Scholar in Britain.

Churchill, upon meeting Humes, said, "Young man, study

history, study history, study history. In history lie all the secrets of statecraft."

Well, I did study history and the collection of historical anecdotes did lead me to a White House speechwriting job. And the use of such anecdotes can lead you to becoming a more powerful speaker. (Incidentally, I went to my room that night and tore down the picture of Ted Williams and put the up a portrait of Churchill.)

One story I posed to Nixon was a story about Churchill at Yalta.

After President Roosevelt offered a flowery toast to Premier Stalin as a lover of peace, the Soviets awaited a toast by Churchill.

Churchill growled in a whisper, "But Stalin does not want peace." But after urging from his staff, he rose and said, "To Premier Stalin, whose conduct of foreign policy manifests a desire for peace." Then away from the translator he muttered, "A piece of Poland, a piece of Czechoslovakia, a piece of Romania . . . "

The reader will note that in this book I devote three sections to anecdotes about Winston Churchill, Abraham Lincoln and Benjamin Franklin.

Churchill, though British (even if half-American), is the leader most corporate captains of industry and commerce most admire, according to *Fortune* magazine.

Lincoln, of course, is the most revered of our presidents. In *Bartlett's Quotations* he is the most extensively quoted of any American.

Franklin, of all of our Founding Fathers, is the most affectionately remembered. Even before the American Revolution, he was the most quoted American. His Poor Richard's sayings had won their way into American hearts.

Each of the three men etch an indelible picture in our

mind's: The bow-tied, cigar-wielding Winston with his bull-dog face, who mobilized the English language and sent it into battle.

The rotund and benign countenance of Ben Franklin, who peered over his spectacles to deliver comic insights into serious matters.

The lanky, awkward "Honest Abe" from whose sad face and wit emerged so many droll and memorable stories.

I hope you will not only find speech material from among the Churchill, Franklin and Lincoln stories, but also from the many other celebrity anecdotes heavily sprinkled throughout these pages.

PART II

Stories and Anecdotes

ABE'S ANECDOTES

Remember that the difference between a joke and humor is that the latter is believable and illustrates a point.

Abraham Lincoln was once asked why he used so much humor in his talks. "I am accused of telling a great many stories," he answered. "They say it lowers the dignity of the presidential office, but I find that people are more easily influenced by a broad, humorous illustration than in any other way and what the hypercritical few may think, I don't care."

Silence

Better to remain silent and be thought a fool than to speak out and remove all doubt.

Common Man

The Lord must prefer the common-looking people, he made so many of them.

Happiness

Most folks are about as happy as they make up their minds to be.

Law

The best way to get a bad law repealed is to enforce it strictly.

Progress

I am a slow walker but I never walk backwards.

Fighter

I can't spare this man—he fights.
[said about U.S. Grant]

Problem

Killing the dog does not cure the bite.

Argument—*Reasons*

I find the reasons pretty thin in this argument. It reminds me of how Abraham Lincoln described the arguments of Stephen Douglas in the famous debate.

"AS THIN AS HOMEOPATHIC SOUP THAT WAS MADE BY BOILING THE SHADOW OF A PIGEON THAT HAD BEEN STARVED TO DEATH."

Improvement—*Competition*

Someone once said that if you stay in the same spot, you will give the advantage to your competitor. At one of the Lincoln-Douglas debates, Senator Stephen Douglas was repeatedly making remarks about Lincoln's lowly station in life and said that his first meeting with him had been across the counter of a general store where liquor was sold. He finally ended his remarks by saying, "And Mr. Lincoln was a very good bartender too."

There was a roar of laughter at this, but it quieted

down considerably when Mr. Lincoln said quietly, "What Mr. Douglas has said, gentlemen, is true enough; I did keep a grocery, and I did sell cotton, candles and cigars, and sometimes whiskey; but I remember in those days that Mr. Douglas was one of my best customers. Many a time have I stood on one side of the counter and sold whiskey to Mr. Douglas on the other side, but the difference between us now is this: I HAVE LEFT MY SIDE OF THE COUNTER, BUT MR. DOUGLAS STILL STICKS TO HIS AS TENACIOUSLY AS EVER."

(Well, looking at the figures, we have advanced on our competition . . .)

Unenthusiasm—*Wary*

I don't like to be negative, so I will avoid comment when I have nothing positive to say. My views are not unlike those of Abraham Lincoln the time an author called at the White House and asked Lincoln to give a plug to his book. Lincoln thought hard and then wrote: "FOR THE SORT OF PEOPLE WHO LIKE THIS BOOK IT IS THE SORT OF BOOK THOSE PEOPLE WILL LIKE."

Purpose—*Direction*

Like Abraham Lincoln I am not sure about everything, but I am sure of one thing—the direction I want to go. When Lincoln ran for Congress in 1846 against Rev. Peter Cartwright, that Methodist hell-fire and damnation evangelist spread the word that Lincoln was godless. Lincoln went to a revival meeting in Springfield, where Cartwright said, "All who do not wish to go to hell will stand." And everybody but Lincoln stood. "I observe that everybody but Mr. Lincoln indicated he did not want to go to hell. May I inquire of you, Mr. Lincoln, where are you going?"

"Brother Cartwright asks me directly where I am going. MY ANSWER IS: I AM GOING TO CONGRESS."

(And I am going to . . .)

Controversy—*Solution*

A good speech, I heard once, offers facts, not furor. It should enlighten the situation, as Abraham Lincoln once explained. In the Civil War Lincoln was disturbed by people who pretended to be wise on a minimum diet of facts. They offered wisdom they did not possess. Lincoln told the story of a backwoods traveler lost in a terrific thunderstorm. The rider floundered through the mud until his horse gave out. Then he stood alone in the middle of the road while lightning streaked and thunder roared around him. One crash seemed to shake the earth underneath, and it brought the traveler to his knees. He cried out, "O LORD, I'M NOT A PRAYING MAN, BUT I'LL MAKE THE PRAYER BRIEF AND TO THE POINT: IF IT'S ALL THE SAME TO YOU, GIVE US A LITTLE MORE LIGHT AND A LITTLE LESS NOISE."

(So let us today try to add some light to a subject that has been noised about by so much controversy lately . . .)

Competitor—*Disadvantage*

If our competitors, in their attempts to expand, want to put themselves in such a stupid position, I'm not going to object. I think of when Lincoln was President and a ranking man in the Post Office died, a job applicant waylaid President Lincoln as he left the White House. "Mr. Lincoln, you know the Chief Postal Inspector just died. Can I take his place?"

"WELL," replied Lincoln, "IT'S ALL RIGHT WITH ME IF IT'S ALL RIGHT WITH THE UNDERTAKER."

Contribution—*Protection*

Ward Lamon, a Springfield lawyer, was a friend and colleague of Lincoln. Just before going to court with Lincoln he ripped the seat of his pants.

Another lawyer passed around a paper, asking for contributions to buy Lamon a new pair of pants. When the paper came around to Lincoln, he wrote, "I CAN CONTRIBUTE NOTHING TO THE END IN VIEW."

(Well, we are not going to be able to cover those who don't cover their ass.)

Underused—*Assets*

For a long while during the Civil War, General McClellan did not fight any battles. Finally, President Lincoln sent him a note:

> My dear McClellan,
>   If you don't want to use the Army, I should like to borrow it for awhile.
>   Yours respectfully,
>   A. Lincoln

(Well, *we* have some underused assets that are not being employed effectively.)

Ego—*Leadership*

Too many top executives act as if they are more interested in their 'perks' than their profits. Ego is their downfall.

When someone saw Abraham Lincoln shining his own shoes in his White House office, the onlooker asked, "Mr. President, why are you blacking your own shoes?"

Lincoln responded, "WHOSE SHOES WOULD YOU HAVE ME BLACK?"

Communication—*Resemblance*

Lincoln's Secretary of State, William Seward, was the most loyal of all the cabinet members even though he had lost the Presidential nomination in 1860 to the lesser-known Illinois lawyer. Once, when often profane Seward was riding with

Lincoln up to the capital, the carriage wheels got stuck in the mud and the driver unleashed a spate of profanity. Lincoln got out of the carriage and asked, "Tell me, driver, what Episcopal church do you go to?"

"What makes you think I'm an Episcopalian?"

"WELL, MR. SEWARD GOES TO THE EPISCOPAL CHURCH AND YOU TALK TO GOD JUST THE WAY HE DOES."

(Well, the Senator calls himself a Republican, but he talks just like a Democrat when he says . . .)

Leadership—*Idiosyncrasies*

During the Civil War, Edmund Stanton, the Secretary of War, told Lincoln of reports from the fields that General Grant was boozing in his tent.

"Find out what kind of whiskey he is drinking."

"Why is that, Mr. President?"

"BECAUSE I WANT TO SEND A CASE OF IT TO MY OTHER GENERALS."

(Well, some people say Bob should quit smoking and lose some weight, but when I look at the job he has done, I'm going to have my personnel people recruit some more fat smokers . . .)

Leadership—*Posture*

It may be difficult to define leadership but Abraham Lincoln knew when someone lacked the courage and judgment that comprises it. Lincoln replaced George McClellan with Joe Hooker in 1864 as head of the Army of the Potomac. Hooker, who tried to clothe himself in the style of a leader, once wrote a memo to Lincoln signed, "From his headquarters in the saddle—Joe Hooker."

Lincoln replied to his staff: "HOOKER SEEMS TO HAVE HIS HEADQUARTERS WHERE HIS HINDQUARTERS OUGHT TO BE."

(What he was saying was that Hooker had his head up his ass—and this might describe the judgment of whomever first advanced this policy.)

Misquotation—*Statement*

That statement that was quoted in the papers was an off-the-top-of-the-head comment. It reminds me of what Abraham Lincoln once said about Stephen Douglas. "When I was a boy," Lincoln said, "I spent considerable time along the Sangamon River. An old steamboat plied on the river, the boiler of which was so small that when they blew the whistle, there wasn't enough steam to turn the paddle wheel. When the paddle wheel went around, they couldn't blow the whistle. "MY FRIEND DOUGLAS," said Lincoln, "REMINDS ME OF THAT OLD STEAMBOAT, FOR IT IS EVIDENT THAT WHEN HE TALKS HE CAN'T THINK, AND WHEN HE THINKS HE CAN'T TALK."

(Well, there was very little thinking involved when that off-the-cuff comment was made.)

Lawyers—*Lawsuit*

There are lawyers that I admire. After all, Abraham Lincoln was one. And Lincoln had this to say about lawyers:

The story goes that in his early years of practicing law, Abraham Lincoln once had to travel across Illinois in midwinter to get to a trial. When he reached the town where the trial was to be held, he checked into the inn next to the courthouse and found the fireplace in the sitting room surrounded by all the other lawyers in town discussing his case.

"Cold out, eh?" remarked one of them.

"Colder than Hell," agreed Lincoln affably.

"You've been there too, Mr. Lincoln?" asked another.

"YUP," he said with a smile, "AND IT'S JUST LIKE HERE—ALL THE LAWYERS ARE STANDING NEXT TO THE FIRE."

(And I might add that our lawyer (or general counsel) might soon be facing a hot time when . . .)

Resourcefulness—*Leadership*

A good leader has the ingenuity to go around obstacles that present themselves.

When Abraham Lincoln was captain of the "Bucktail" Rangers in 1832, he was as ignorant of military matters as his company was of drill and tactics. On one occasion, his troop, marching in platoon formation, was confronted by a fence. Captain Lincoln had no idea of the proper order, but his quick wit did not desert him. "Company dismissed for two minutes," he commanded. "AT THE END OF THAT TIME, FALL IN AND ON THE OTHER SIDE OF THE FENCE."

(Similarly, we intend to get around the problem by . . .)

Honor—*Assignment*

Lincoln, after an evening at the White House, was asked, "How does it feel to be President of the United States?"

"You have heard," said Lincoln, "about the man tarred and feathered and ridden out of town on a rail? A man in the crowd asked him how he liked it, and his reply was, 'IF IT WASN'T FOR THE HONOR OF THE THING, I WOULD RATHER WALK.'"

(But like Lincoln, I know it is a paramount responsibility ahead of me . . .)

Congress—*Mess*

Senator Ben Wade led a delegation to the White House to register their complaints. "Mr. President Wade said, this administration is going right to perdition. Why, it's only a mile away from Hell right now."

And Lincoln replied, "WELL, SENATOR THAT'S JUST ABOUT THE DISTANCE OF THE WHITE HOUSE TO CAPITOL HILL."

(Well, it is Congress that has gotten us into the mess we face . . .)

Background—*Family*

A story is told about the Lincoln-Douglas debates in 1858. At one of them, Senator Douglas was introduced with a fulsome tribute to his distinguished forebears and the eminence of his family. When he finished, Lincoln rose without an introduction and began: "I ONLY KNOW THIS ABOUT MY ANCESTRY: I COME FROM A LONG LINE OF MARRIED FOLKS."

Sell-Out—*Expediency*

Gentlemen, we can either do the hard thing or the easy, the right or the wrong. But I don't feel like buying a lightning rod for an uneasy conscience like Abraham Lincoln's one-time foe.

In Lincoln's campaign for re-election to the Illinois legislature, he tangled in debate with one George Forquer, a onetime Whig who had changed his politics to Democrat in order to receive a handsome appointment from President Jackson. Forquer had also just recently built a new home, topped with a lightning rod. In the debate, Forquer ridiculed and brutally attacked the young Lincoln. When it was Lincoln's turn to speak he replied to Forquer's argument clearly and effectively. Then he paused and with cutting sarcasm launched an attack on his opponent.

"Among other things, my opponent in this debate has said that 'this young man,' alluding to me, 'must be taken down.' I am not so young in years as I am in tricks of the trade of a politician, but," Lincoln said, pointing a deadly finger at Forquer, "LIVE LONG OR DIE YOUNG, I WOULD RATHER DIE NOW THAN, LIKE THE GENTLEMAN, CHANGE MY POLITICS AND WITH IT RECEIVE AN OFFICE WORTH THREE THOUSAND DOLLARS A YEAR AND THEN FEEL OBLIGED TO

ERECT A LIGHTNING ROD OVER MY HOUSE TO PROTECT A GUILTY CONSCIENCE FROM AN OFFENDED GOD."

(Well, today, if we stand by our principles, there is only one way to answer this challenge.)

Claim—*Reality*

Some of Lincoln's advisors told him to issue a proclamation saying that all the slaves were free. Lincoln insisted that saying slaves were free would not make them free. To explain, he asked, "If you call a sheep's tail a leg, how many legs does a sheep have?"

"Five," the advisors agreed.

"No," replied Lincoln. "A SHEEP ONLY HAS FOUR LEGS." Then Lincoln said, "CALLING A TAIL A LEG DOESN'T MAKE IT SO."

(Well, our competitor can make outrageous claims but the truth is . . .)

Cost—*Inflation*

Lincoln once attended a church bazaar as president. Buying a bunch of violets, he gave the lady at the booth a twenty-dollar bill. She made no attempt to make change and gushed, "Oh, thank you, Mr. President."

At this Lincoln reached down from his great height, gently touched the woman's wrist and asked, "What do you call this?"

"Why, Mr. President, that is my wrist. What did you think it was?"

Replied Lincoln, "WELL, I THOUGHT IT MIGHT BE YOUR ANKLE. EVERYTHING ELSE IS SO HIGH AROUND HERE."

(Frankly, the rise of costs is imperiling our operation.)

Background—*Autobiography*

Since I am asked to say something about my background, I am reminded of what Abraham Lincoln said when he was asked by a newspaper to write the story of his life upon being nominated in 1860. He replied, "It is contained in one line of Gray's *Elegy Written in a Country Church-Yard:* 'THE SHORT AND SIMPLE ANNALS OF THE POOR.'"

Advice—*Criticism*

Abraham Lincoln once regaled his Cabinet with the story of the king who wanted the weather foretold, so he found a stable boy who could do it. Each day, upon the king's request, the lad would leave the palace for a time and then come back with the correct prognostication after a short while. Being curious, the king decided to have the boy followed. He learned that the boy went to a stable and asked a donkey if the weather was to be fair. If it was, the donkey's ears would go forward. If not, they would point backward. The king, upon this discovery, made the donkey Prime Minister.

"BUT THE PROBLEM WAS," summarized Lincoln, "THAT THE FIRST THING YOU KNEW, EVERY JACKASS WANTED TO BE PRIME MINISTER."

(We are beset by too many advisors telling us what we should or shouldn't do. Some of the half-assed criticism we are hearing . . .)

Leadership—*Flattery*

How many of us speak frankly to our bosses? Is it because we fear they would resent anything that could be construed as criticism?

Justice Oliver Wendell Holmes served in the Civil War. In 1864, a contingent of Confederate cavalry stormed into Washington. In the short skirmish that followed, Captain Holmes saw a man standing in the Confederate line of fire. Not knowing it was President Lincoln, Holmes screamed, "Will that damn fool in the stovepipe hat get down!" The President quickly obeyed.

Later, Lincoln came over to thank the embarrassed Holmes. The President added, "FINALLY, SOMEONE WHO KNOWS HOW TO SPEAK STRAIGHT TO HIS PRESIDENT."

(A real leader wants straight talk and . . .)

Study—*Investigation*

One time during the war a Senator came to President Lincoln because his brother-in-law was in danger of losing his government patronage job. It seems he had been caught looking over the window transom on a hotel door in Washington while a visiting French actress was disrobing.

"WELL, SENATOR," Lincoln told him, "I WAS THINKING OF PROMOTING HIM TO A PEERAGE."

(Well, I think some recognition should be given to our colleague who has looked into the problem of . . .)

Reorganization—*Dismissal*

During the Civil War, President Lincoln dismissed one member of his Cabinet. A political ally then suggested he fire the whole Cabinet. Lincoln responded that it reminded him of a farmer he knew in Illinois who was bothered by skunks. "I SHOT ONE SKUNK," the farmer said, "AND IT RAISED SUCH A STINK THAT I LET THE OTHER SEVEN GO."

(Well, any talk of complete reorganization and wholesale shifting of executive personnel is not true. Not only because it would raise a stink, but because we have some pretty able executives who . . .)

BEN'S BELLY LAUGHS

Cash

There are three faithful friends—an old wife, an old dog and ready cash.

Criticism

Don't throw stones at your neighbors if your own windows are glass.

Experience

Experience keeps a dear school but fools will learn in no other.

Life

I have no objection to a repetition of my life from its beginning only asking the advantages authors have in a second edition to correct its faults.

Marriage

Keep your eyes wide open before marriage, afterwards keep them half shut.

Where there's marriage without love, there will be love without marriage.

Politician

Here comes the orator with his flood of words and drop of reason.

Weariness

After three days, men grow weary of a wench, a guest and weather rainy.

Advertising—*Public Relations*

The story is told about Ben Franklin at the Continental Congress in Philadelphia. After the Declaration of Independence was signed, President John Hancock said, "Dr. Franklin, your country needs you." Franklin replied, "I'm too old to be a soldier." "No," said Hancock, "we want you to be Minister to France."

"Well, that's fine," chuckled Franklin. "SOLDIERS HAVE TO DIE FOR THEIR COUNTRY BUT DIPLOMATS ONLY HAVE TO LIE FOR THEIR COUNTRY."

(Well, promoting a country or a product does involve a lot of puffery but in our case the facts will speak for themselves without any frills.)

Danger—*Risks*

While the proposal has some obvious advantages, it does place us in a dangerous situation.

At the Constitutional Convention, Franklin opposed the proposed Standing Army provision. He was worried that it would be like "a President's police force," and believed that any armed forces should be authorized by vote of Congress. Franklin helped defeat the provision by arguing, "A STANDING ARMY IS LIKE AN ERECTION. WHILE IT MAY ENHANCE DOMESTIC HARMONY AND CONJUGAL RELATIONS, IT ALSO INVITES TEMPTATION FOR FOREIGN ADVENTURES."

(Similarly the dangers may outweigh the advantages.)

Modernization—*Decline*

Management that doesn't adapt to changing times carries the seeds of decline.

Before the Revolutionary War, Benjamin Franklin lobbied in London for revisions of tax laws. He paid visits to fellow writers whose views might be more sympathetic to the American position. He met David Hume, the Scottish philosopher and writer of British history, who issued a ringing support of the colonies. But then Franklin called on the eminent historian, Edward Gibbon, who had just written *Decline and Fall of the Roman Empire*. Gibbon wouldn't receive him, saying from the other side of the door, "I decline to associate with anyone who would dishonor my king."

Franklin answered back, "THAT'S A PITY. I WAS GOING TO OFFER YOU MY HELP ON THE WRITING OF A SEQUEL—*Decline and Fall of the British Empire.*"

(If we don't modernize and update our management, we will face a decline.)

Unity

When the Continental Congress voted in 1776 for the Resolves for Independence, President John Hancock warned delegates, "We better all hang together." Benjamin Franklin replied, "WE BETTER HANG TOGETHER OR MOST ASSUREDLY WE WILL ALL HANG SEPARATELY."

Taxes—*Impact*

When Franklin served as the colonies' representative in London, the king's prime minister, Lord Townshend, asked him to read over the proposed Stamp Act and comment on it. Franklin did and told the British minister that it was fine—if he would make one little change. Townshend was surprised that Franklin seemed so agreeable and asked him what it was. "Oh," said Franklin, "just change the word *one* to *two.*"

When Townshend reread the bill, he exploded to Franklin: "If we change to *two* the only *one* in the bill it would mean that the statute would become operative not in 1774 but 2774."

Replied Franklin, "YOU FIGURE RIGHT."

(Unfortunately, some of the taxes proposed will take place now—not centuries in the future.)

Loss—*Deficit*

The story is told of a ball that Minister Franklin attended in Versailles. Many of the lovely countesses and French ladies attending adorned their bosoms with Wedgewood cameo lockets bearing Franklin's image. While Franklin was with King Louis, one rather scrawny lady came up to purr over Franklin. When she left, the king commented, "It's a pity, Franklin, she does not do justice to her decolletage. God did not endow her."

"YES," said Franklin, "BUT YOU, SIRE, ON THE OTHER HAND, CAN ENDOW US, FOR OUR GOVERNMENT IN PHILADELPHIA, LIKE THE UNFORTUNATE LADY IN QUESTION, HAS THE SAME PROBLEM—AN UNCOVERED DEFICIT."

(We have some losses that have to be soon covered.)

Facts—Controversy

Four years before his death, Benjamin Franklin received word from a mayor of a Massachusetts town. The town wished to rename itself after the Massachusetts native who had become the world's most revered statesman. In their letter the town council proclaimed its plan to erect a bell tower in Franklin's honor.

Franklin wrote back that he was honored by their decision to name their town after him. But he said he wished that the money that would be spent for the tower and the bell be used instead for the establishment of a library. Franklin added in a postscript, "I PREFER BOOKS TO BELLS AND SENSE TO SOUND."

(Well, there has been much controversy surrounding this incident and it is time to bring some facts to the furor.)

Modification—Proposal

Sometimes a proposal needs a second look. In history we remember how the Constitutional Convention was deadlocked on the issue of representation—whether there should be the same number of representatives for each state or whether it should be determined by population. Benjamin

Franklin supported the idea of having both a House and Senate as a compromise.

To those who questioned the idea of having two legislative houses, Franklin made them chuckle with his tale about a man who had recently visited General Washington in Philadelphia. The visitor, when taking coffee, filled his saucer with it before pouring it into his cup. When the general asked him why, the visitor answered, "To cool off the coffee." And Washington replied, "THAT'S WHY WE NEED A SENATE—THE SENATE IS THE SAUCER: IT CAN COOL OFF WHAT THE HOUSE COOKS UP!"

(Similarly, we may have to modify some of the proposals.)

Neutrality—*Involvement*

I must admit difficulty in hiding my contempt for those who won't get involved and won't commit themselves. I find myself in sympathy with Benjamin Franklin when, in 1776, he sailed to the court of Versailles to try to persuade France to support the American colonies in their war against Britain. King Louis hated England but was reluctant to assist an effort to topple a monarch. At a formal state dinner King Louis said, "Dr. Franklin, our chef has gone to great length to prepare this chicken recipe—his pièce de resistance—his roast capon?"

"No," replied Franklin. "I DECLINE TO HAVE ANYTHING TO DO WITH NEUTERED ANIMALS."

Authoritarian—*Dictatorial*

Benjamin Franklin had another run-in with the French King Louis XVI on his 1776 trip to France to try to persuade the King to support the American cause. Franklin could have said he wasn't really opposed to the monarchy, that his country was just fighting for its independence. But right from the start he made his anti-king position clear.

In one of his first visits to the king, Franklin was invited to play chess. As the table was being set up, Franklin took the two king pieces off the board. To the startled monarch, Franklin flashed an impish smile and said, "IN AMERICA, WE HAVE NO NEED FOR KINGS."

(Well, in management we have no use for authoritarian or dictatorial techniques . . .)

Private Enterprise—*Businessman*

When Benjamin Franklin was Postmaster General of the colonies his frank was *B. Franklin Free*. When the colonies declared their independence, the new United States made him Postmaster General. As the war with Britain loomed, Franklin changed his logo to *B. Free Franklin*.

(America's first small businessman to make himself a fortune was Franklin. Today, he would have fought against the tyranny of taxes and regulation by red tape.)

Appearances—*Surprise*

We must be careful not to judge by appearances. Take it from this story about Benjamin Franklin.

Benjamin Franklin was a little stout later in life and it was said that in Paris a young woman, tapping him on his protruding abdomen, said, "Dr. Franklin, if this were on a woman, we'd know what to think."

And Franklin replied, "HALF AN HOUR AGO, MADEMOISELLE, IT WAS ON A WOMAN, AND NOW WHAT DO YOU THINK?"

Chaos—*Politicians*

In the 1780's, the new nation called the United States was floundering, with tariffs between the states bigger than those between European countries and salaries for the national postoffice workers often suspended. It was during this time that Benjamin Franklin entertained Dr. Benjamin

Rush and Thomas Jefferson. The subject of conversation turned to trying to determine what was the oldest profession.

Dr. Rush, a physician, said the oldest profession was his. "You see, it was a surgical operation that made Eve out of Adam's rib."

But Jefferson, who built Monticello, said, "No, it was the architect. After all it was an architect who brought the world out of chaos."

Then replied Franklin, "YOU'RE BOTH WRONG. IT'S THE POLITICIAN. AFTER ALL WHO DO YOU THINK CREATED THE CHAOS?"

(The chaos we find ourselves in today may not be completely the fault of politicians but . . .)

Replacement—*Honoree*

When Thomas Jefferson presented his credentials as U.S. minister to France, the French premier remarked, "I see that you have come to replace Benjamin Franklin." Jefferson corrected him. "NO ONE CAN REPLACE DR. FRANKLIN. I AM ONLY SUCCEEDING HIM."

(Well, our honoree tonight is irreplaceable.)

Office—*Promotion*

John Hancock, the President of the Continental Congress, welcomed Benjamin Franklin back from England in 1775 with the news. "Dr. Franklin, we're giving you your old job back as Postmaster General of the Colonies."

Chuckled Franklin, "I NEVER SEEK, I NEVER REFUSE, I NEVER RESIGN AN OFFICE."

(Well, now that I have this new job you are going to have a hard time getting me out.)

Gratitude—*Age*

If Benjamin Franklin was an author of liberty, he was also an authority on love. He preferred the charms of older women because as he said:

"THEY DON'T TELL
THEY DON'T YELL
THEY DON'T SWELL
AND THEY'RE GRATEFUL AS HELL."

(Well, I won't comment on that but as an older woman—I "will tell" that I am very grateful that . . .)

Guarantees—*Opportunity*

We all know there is no free lunch—no guarantee of benefits and rewards without work and planning. Benjamin Franklin, with his sagacity and wit, expressed that to a heckler. During the early days of the American Republic, he spoke many times on that great document, the Declaration of Independence. After one such stirring speech an uncouth fellow rose and boldly walked a few paces toward the platform. "Aw, them words don't mean nothin' a-tall!" he shouted at Franklin. "Where's all the happiness you say it guarantees us?"

Franklin smiled benevolently at the questioner and quickly replied, "MY FRIEND, THE DECLARATION ONLY GUARANTEES THE AMERICAN PEOPLE THE RIGHT TO PURSUE HAPPINESS. YOU HAVE TO CATCH IT YOURSELF!"

(The opportunity for fulfillment is before us, but we must answer the challenge.)

Diplomacy—*Compromise*

There is a right way and a wrong way in management. Forcing what you want down someone's throat is the wrong way.

In 1753, Ben Franklin was called to a British general staff

meeting at Carlisle. General Braddock was telling a Virginia colonel named George Washington that he couldn't understand why the German farmers would not give him their wagons to help the British fight the French. With his face as red as his tunic, Braddock blustered, "I have half a mind to take those wagons at the point of a musket."

Franklin replied, "WELL, GENERAL, YOU'RE RIGHT ABOUT ONE THING—YOUR MIND!"

Franklin persuaded Braddock to rent the wagons. The Germans made a profit and the British got their wagons.

Honoree—*Rescuer*

In Versailles, during the negotiations of the Revolution, the freed American colonies were still not treated like a nation. There was even one banquet to which no American diplomats were invited.

After the American Revolutionary War, Benjamin Franklin, the English ambassador and the French minister were dining together. They agreed that each should offer a toast.

The French minister began: "To His Majesty, Louis the Sixteenth, who, like the sun, fills the earth with a soft, benevolent glow."

The English ambassador followed with: "To George the Third, who, like the moon, spreads his light and illuminates the world."

Then Franklin barged into the banquet, making his way to the head table and raising his glass: "TO GENERAL GEORGE WASHINGTON, THE JOSHUA, WHO STOPPED THE SUN AND MOON IN THEIR TRACKS."

(Today we are here to honor one who has made the whole world stop and take notice . . .)

Program—*Endorsement*

Most speeches offer programs; mine tonight will be no exception. Now audiences naturally want to be aware of all the implications that might arise from the adoption of the program. The effects, I can assure you, will be far better than those foreseen in an incident in the English Parliament two hundred years ago. At the time of our War of Independence, there was a rebellious member of the House of Commons named John Wilkes. Now Wilkes took delight in supporting his friend, Benjamin Franklin and the American cause, much to the consternation of the Tory government. Wilkes and Franklin both were members of an early swinging club named the Hell Fire Club.

One day, after a speech that seemed treasonable to the Tory hierarchy, Wilkes found himself attacked by a member of the front bench, Lord Sandwich. Sandwich said, "The honorable gentleman who consorts with the traitor and rogue Franklin will have a limited career in this chamber, for it shall either end on the gallows or by a loathsome disease."

Wilkes coolly replied: "THE HONORABLE LORD MAY WELL BE CORRECT. IT ALL DEPENDS ON WHETHER I EMBRACE HIS PROGRAMS OR EMBRACE HIS MISTRESS."

(Well tonight, although I don't have any mistress for you to embrace, I do have a program . . .)

Costs—*Competition*

I remember from studying history, the story of a small company that was facing tough economic times. Back in Philadelphia, Benjamin Franklin's print shop was being threatened by a group of the city's leaders who had decided that Franklin ought to be taken down a peg. They cut him out of all government contracts, both city and state. Franklin in retaliation sent out engraved invitations to the ten city fathers to come to his house. Out of curiosity they came.

At each place was set a bowl of something that looked like dry, gray mush. Franklin, at the head of the table, took a pitcher of water, added some to his bowl and then proceeded to wolf down the contents greedily.

One of the guests then poured some water into his bowl and tried a spoonful. He quickly spat it out, saying, "Franklin, what the devil is in this bowl?"

Franklin replied, "PLAIN OLD SAWDUST. AND IF YOU UNDERSTAND THAT I CAN LIVE OFF THAT AND LIKE IT, YOU OUGHT TO KNOW THAT YOU'LL NEVER SQUEEZE ME OUT OF MY BUSINESS."

(Well, we plan some not so harsh cost-cutting plans that will make our competition understand . . .)

Packaging—*Advertising*

Benjamin Franklin was an inventor. One of his most noteworthy was the Franklin stove, which retained heat and didn't make the whole kitchen a boiler room. Accordingly, it was a more efficient and exact instrument for baking and cooking.

As a businessman he marketed it in his *Pennsylvania Almanac* as "a stove whose heat would not dry out the complexions of fair ladies." It was an immediate success.

(So, the question before us is, how we shall market our new product to the consumer.)

WIT OF WINSTON

Alcohol

All I can say is that I have taken more out of alcohol than alcohol has taken out of me.

Brandy

Good cognac is like a woman. Do not assault it. Coddle and warm it in your hands before you gently sip it.

Defeat

Although always prepared for martyrdom, I prefer that it shall be postponed.

Democracy

Democracy's the worst form of government except for every other form that's been tried from time-to-time.

Enjoyment

If this is a world of vice and woe, I'll take the vice and you have the woe.

Exercise

I get my exercise being a pall-bearer for those of my friends who believed in regular running and calisthenics.

Facts

You must look at the facts because they look at you.

Free Enterprise

It is a socialist idea that making a profit is a vice—the real vice is making a loss.

Life

Do what you like but remember—like what you do.

Middle Age

The young sow wild oats. The old grow sage.

Tobacco

Smoking a cigar is like falling in love. First you choose it for its shape. Then you stay with it for its flavor. But you must remember: never, never let the flame go out.

Vice

Do not trust a man who has not a single redeeming vice.

Perfection—*Change*

In 1900, the newly elected Winston Churchill made a speaking tour in America. In Washington, he was introduced to a very beautiful woman from Richmond, Virginia, who prided herself on her devotion to the lost cause of the Confederacy. Her family had opposed the North's policy of Reconstruction.

Anxious that Churchill should know her sentiments, she remarked as she gave him her hand, "Mr. Churchill, you see before you a rebel who has not been reconstructed."

"MADAM," he replied with a deep bow, "RECONSTRUCTION IN YOUR CASE WOULD BE BLASPHEMOUS."

(Similarly, I see no reason why we should change our . . .)

Award—*Reciprocity*

In 1946 Winston Churchill went to Fulton, Missouri, to deliver his famous Iron Curtain Address. A ceremony was held before the speech to dedicate a bust of the wartime prime minister. After the speech, a buxom belle barged up to Churchill and gushed, "Mr. Churchill, I traveled over a hundred miles this morning for the unveiling of your bust."

Replied the gallant Churchill, "MADAM, I ASSURE YOU, IN THAT REGARD I WOULD GLADLY RETURN THE FAVOR."

(Although I won't be able to return the favor that way, I would like to extend . . .)

Criticism—*Stupidity*

My reaction to the criticism of that particular party is much the same as that of Winston Churchill when one day in the House of Commons, a Socialist poured out abusive words against the prime minister. Churchill remained impassive—almost bored.

When the harangue was over, Churchill rose and said, "IF I VALUED THE OPINION OF THE HONORABLE GENTLEMAN, I MIGHT GET ANGRY."

Repeat—*Second Chance*

In the 1930's, when Churchill had become unpopular for urging rearming because of Hitler, George Bernard Shaw sent him two tickets to the opening night of one of his plays, along with the message, "Dear Winston: Here are two tickets; bring a friend if you have one."

Winston returned the tickets with the note, "Dear G.B.S.: Unfortunately, a prior engagement prevents my attending opening night. BUT I WOULD LIKE A TICKET FOR THE SECOND NIGHT—IF THERE IS ONE."

(Well, I am happy that you have given me a second chance . . .)

Choice—*Option*

One of the worst excuses anyone can make for a policy gone wrong is to say there was no other way. The highest responsibility for a decision-maker is to examine all alternatives. We remember the story about Winston Churchill who at a reception in Canada in 1931 found himself next to the stiff-necked Methodist Bishop of Calgary.

A young woman appeared with a tray of sherry glasses. She offered one to Churchill, which he took, and then to the Methodist bishop. The bishop was aghast at the alcoholic offer saying, "Young lady, I'd rather commit adultery than take an intoxicating beverage."

Thereupon, Sir Winston said, "COME BACK HERE, LASSIE; I DIDN'T KNOW WE HAD A CHOICE."

(Well, we do have a choice before us, in fact, we have several options to consider . . .)

Defeat—*Disorganization*

On the day of the British general election in 1922, Winston Churchill was convalescing from an appendicitis operation. The attack had stopped short his campaigning. In addition to this handicap, the Liberal Party, to which he belonged, had been badly split by dissenting factions. When the returns came in, Churchill was in a hospital listening to a new contraption called the "wireless." He shook his head sadly at the reports of the landslide defeat of his party and murmured, "ALL OF A SUDDEN, I FIND MYSELF WITHOUT A PARTY, WITHOUT A MINISTRY AND WITHOUT A SEAT AND EVEN WITHOUT AN APPENDIX."

(So although I still have an appendix, I find myself, like Churchill, part of an organization that is being disbanded and troops that are being dismissed . . .)

Summons—*Emergency*

In the early days of the blitz, Winston Churchill motored hurriedly to Canterbury to see that proper precautions were taken for the protection of the famous cathedral there. Later he explained to the Archbishop, "We have bolstered the edifice and approaches with sandbags to spare. Every device known to man has been applied. No matter how many close hits the Nazis may make, I feel sure the cathedral will survive."

"Ah, yes, close hits," said the Archbishop gloomily, "but what if they score a direct hit upon us?"

"IN THAT EVENT," decided Churchill with some asperity, "YOU WILL HAVE TO REGARD IT, MY DEAR ARCHBISHOP, AS A SUMMONS."

(Well, sudden events have issued us a summons and we must answer the situation.)

Improvement—*Youth*

As I look at the young people who make up this audience, I think of how in only a few years, you who are today's students will be tomorrow's shapers of our society. Your future role recalls the story about the late Sir Winston Churchill.

It was in 1955, when Churchill was at the sunset of his life. He was accustomed to spending most of his time in the antechambers where liquid refreshments were dispensed. On one occasion, the bell rang for a division vote and Churchill, thoroughly fortified, began to wobble toward the door as the 250-pound Laborite from Liverpool, Bessie Braddock, came waddling toward the same door. There was the inevitable collision between the wobbler and the waddler and down went Bessie for the count.

Furious, Bessie got herself off the floor, mad as a hornet, and said, "Sir Winston, you are drunk. Furthermore, you are disgracefully drunk."

Churchill looked at the obese Bessie and replied, "MRS. BRADDOCK, YOU ARE UGLY. FURTHERMORE, YOU ARE DISGRACEFULLY UGLY. WHAT'S MORE, TOMORROW I, WINSTON CHURCHILL, SHALL BE SOBER."

(Today you may be the students, but tomorrow will find you assuming a leadership role in all walks of society . . .)

(Note: I first brought this story back to the United States in 1959 and since then it has been told countlessly, often with the elegant Lady Astor being mistakenly substituted for Bessie Braddock as the recipient of the Churchill retort.)

Honor—*Appreciation*

As I accept this honor, I think of an incident involving the late Sir Winston Churchill. A prominent Virginia woman had the honor of entertaining the former prime minister at a British War Bond rally in Richmond, Virginia. Since Churchill was arriving by train from Washington on Sunday to deliver a major luncheon address the next day, the woman decided on an informal Sunday night supper with a fare of cold fried chicken and champagne.

On the night of the dinner, the hostess, a woman of Rubenesque proportions, was offering her distinguished guest some chicken. Churchill asked for a breast. The hostess reprimanded him, saying in her southern drawl, "Mr. Churchill, in this part of the country nice people don't use that word. They say white meat."

The next day a florist made a delivery to the hostess' apartment. She opened the box and found an orchid corsage. With the flower was Churchill's card with the inscription: "I'D BE MOST OBLIGED IF YOU WOULD PIN THIS ON YOUR WHITE MEAT."

(I would like to handout some bouquets to people who were responsible for my success.)

Difficulty—*Progress*

After the recent decline I tend to view any success, however small, as a measure of progress. It's like the time Churchill as, Leader of the Opposition, took sick. During the illness his trained nurse heard him chuckling as she left the room bearing a bedpan. She said, "Mr. Churchill, I don't see anything funny about taking out a bedpan." Replied Churchill, "IT'S NOT YOU. I'M CONGRATULATING MYSELF. IT'S THE FIRST TIME A MOVEMENT I'VE BACKED HAS BEEN CARRIED OUT SINCE THE SOCIALIST GOVERNMENT CAME IN."

Criticism—*Mediocrity*

All criticism has to be judged by its source. In this case I think a detailed answer to the charges is no more called for than the time a Socialist named Denis Palings attacked Winston Churchill in the House of Commons. (Paling is a word that means a high spiked fence upon which you can be impaled. Such a fence exists around the House of Commons and the White House.) The Socialist member called Churchill "an exponent of dirty-dog capitalism" ("dirty dog" being a term much like "yellow dog," which we use to describe certain types of contracts or journalism.)

Now Palings, who had served as a deputy Postmaster General in the Socialist government, was really not a worthy foe for the great Churchill. But Sir Winston replied in this fashion: "I WILL NOT ANSWER THE GENTLEMAN'S ATTACK. IT IS ALREADY TOO CLEAR WHAT A DIRTY DOG DOES TO PALINGS."

(Similarly I feel no need to reply to . . .)

Action—*Delay*

I, for one, am anxious to start. I know the feeling of restlessness Winston Churchill often had. One particular time during World War II he worked far into the night without maintaining even a pretense of a schedule. In sharp contrast, General Bernard Montgomery, Britain's top army commander, retired early and kept regular hours. Once, when the two were conferring in Montgomery's headquarters, the general glanced at his watch at 10:00 P.M. and observed, with a suggestion of weariness, "It's past my bedtime. Why don't we call a halt?"

Reluctantly, Churchill agreed. In the morning when they met again the Prime Minister inquired, "Do you feel rested now?"

"No," answered Montgomery. "I have a headache. I didn't sleep enough."

"I HAVE A HEADACHE, TOO," declared Churchill. "I SLEPT TOO MUCH."

(Now, it is not the time to rest on our success . . .)

Bureaucracy—*Regulations 1*

In the gentleman's lavatory in the British House of Commons there is, or was, a very long urinal with a great row of appliances. One day, Clement Attlee, a leader of the Labour Party, was addressing a urinal near the door, when Winston Churchill entered and walked all the way to the other end of the room to do his business. Said Mr. Attlee, "Winston, I know we're political opponents, but we don't have to carry our differences into the gentleman's lavatory."

Mr. Churchill replied, "CLEMENT, THE TROUBLE WITH YOU SOCIALISTS IS THAT WHENEVER YOU SEE ANYTHING IN GOOD WORKING CONDITION YOU WANT THE GOVERNMENT TO REGULATE IT."

Support—*Help*

When Churchill was first a candidate in 1900, he did some door-to-door canvassing. Things were going pretty well, he thought, until he came to the house of a grouchy-looking fellow. After Churchill introduced himself, the fellow said, "Vote for you? Why, I'd rather vote for the Devil!"

"I UNDERSTAND," replied Churchill. "BUT IN CASE YOUR FRIEND IS NOT RUNNING, MAY I COUNT ON YOUR SUPPORT?"

Report—*Profitable*

A young member of Parliament delivered a speech at a banquet which Churchill attended. Afterwards the young man asked the great orator to rate his own effort.

Churchill replied, "FIRST, YOU READ THE SPEECH. SEC-ONDLY, YOU READ IT BADLY, FINALLY IT WASN'T A SPEECH WORTH READING!"

(Well, I am going to read my report but I think you will find the record of growth and profit at least worth listening to.)

Speech—*Talk*

A reporter once asked the old statesman what in his life did he find the most difficult test. Churchill replied, "To CLIMB A LADDER LEANING TOWARDS YOU. TO KISS A GIRL LEANING AWAY FROM YOU AND THIRD, TO GIVE AN AFTER-DINNER SPEECH."

Committee—*Inaction*

When Churchill visited New York in the early 1930's, he was taken to his first American football game at Columbia University. When he was asked for his comment on the game, he replied, "ACTUALLY, IT IS SOMEWHAT LIKE RUGBY. BUT WHY DO YOU HAVE TO HAVE ALL THOSE COMMITTEE MEETINGS?"

Finance—*Budget*

At a diplomatic reception in London before the First World War, an Italian military attaché noticed a medal worn by the Luxembourg ambassador. He asked about it. The Luxembourg diplomat replied stiffly that it was for an ancient order called the Royal Admiralty Cross. The Italian diplomat then remarked to Churchill, who was then First Lord of the Admiralty in Britain, "Mr. Churchill, can you believe that they have an Admiralty award and they don't even have a Navy?"

Churchill replied, "Why shouldn't they have an Admiralty? YOU, AFTER ALL, HAVE A MINISTRY OF FINANCE—YET YOU DON'T HAVE A TREASURY."

(Well, we won't have much of a treasury if we do not cut some costs . . .)

Investment—*Capitalization*

A year after he was voted out of office in 1945, Churchill came on a visit to the United States. In Washington, he boarded the private train *The Ferdinand Magellan* with President Harry Truman for the trip to Missouri, where Churchill would deliver his famous Iron Curtain Address. During the night on the train, Churchill was introduced to the game of poker by Truman and his military aide, General Harry Vaughan. Losing steadily during the night, Churchill looked at the big pot with only a pair of jacks in his hand. Staring back and forth at Truman and Vaughan, he grumbled aloud, "SHOULD I WAGER BRITAIN'S PRECIOUS STERLING ON A COUPLE OF KNAVES?"

The double bluff worked and Truman and Vaughan folded.

(But today I question whether we, with such slim assets, should risk . . .)

Conference—*Arrangements*

As a young man, Churchill was asked by his friend about the London dinner party he had attended the night before:

"WELL," replied Churchill, "IT WOULD HAVE BEEN SPLENDID . . . IF THE WINE HAD BEEN AS COLD AS THE SOUP, THE BEEF AS RARE AS THE SERVICE, THE BRANDY AS OLD AS THE FISH, AND THE MAID AS WILLING AS THE DUCHESS."

(Fortunately for us the arrangements for the meeting [or conference] . . .)

Disaster—*Escape*

We are fortunate to have escaped the consequences for what might have been a disaster. I recall once when Churchill attacked Nancy Astor for being an "appeaser" of Hitler. He found himself later that day at Cliveden, the country house of Lady Astor. When coffee was served, the acid-tongued Nancy, in pouring it, said, "Winston, if I were your wife, I'd put poison in your coffee."

"NANCY," Churchill replied to the lady member of Parliament, "IF I WERE YOUR HUSBAND, I'D DRINK IT."

(Well, I don't know what radical action we would have had to take if we had stayed on that course. Fortunately . . .)

Concealment—*Openness*

During Churchill's first visit to the White House, the British prime minister was surprised one morning by an unexpected visit by President Roosevelt to his bedroom. F.D.R., propelling himself in his wheelchair, found his guest stark naked and gleaming pink from his bath. Faced with this vision the American president put his chair into reverse. But Churchill stopped him, saying, "PRAY ENTER. HIS MAJESTY'S FIRST MINISTER HAS NOTHING TO HIDE FROM THE PRESIDENT OF THE UNITED STATES."

(Like Churchill, we have nothing to hide in this matter.)

Team—*Ally*

When Churchill returned to 10 Downing Street in 1951, he soon scheduled a trip to inspect the N.A.T.O. defenses. On his way by plane to meet the head of Cyprus, Archbishop Makarios, he asked his defense minister, Harold Macmillan, what kind of man the Archbishop was. "Is he one of those priestly ascetics concerned only with spiritual grace or one of those crafty prelates concerned rather with temporal gain?"

"Regrettably," replied Macmillan, "the Archbishop seems to be one of the latter."

"GOOD," replied Churchill, rubbing his hands. "HE IS ONE OF OUR KIND, AND WE CAN WORK TOGETHER."

(Our friend is one who is interested in profit and gain and we are proud to be working with . . .)

Future—*Unlikelihood*

When Churchill first served in the House of Commons in 1900, he grew a moustache to better resemble his late father, Lord Randolph. He also began to vote very independently. A woman contemporary was less than enthusiastic about the new Churchill. "Winston," she scolded when she encountered him at a dinner party, "I neither approve your new politics or your new moustache."

"MADAM," replied Winston, "YOU ARE NOT LIKELY TO COME IN CONTACT WITH EITHER."

(Well, there are a lot of things that could happen in the future that concern us. But one thing that doesn't is . . .)

Bargain—*Productivity*

When the first destroyers arrived in the fall of 1940 under America's Lend-Lease program to Great Britain, Prime Minister Churchill went to inspect them. He was joined by F.D.R.'s right-hand man, Harry Hopkins. Churchill, looking at the decidedly overaged ships, grumbled in a whisper, "Cheap and nasty." Hopkins, who was startled by the remark, queried, "What was that?"

Churchill amended aloud, "CHEAP FOR US AND NASTY FOR THE GERMANS."

(It seems that we have secured at bargain cost something that will increase our productivity.)

Age—*Retirement*

While sitting on a platform waiting to speak, the seventy-eight year-old Churchill was handed a note by an aide. Churchill glanced at the message, which advised: "Prime Minister—your fly is unbuttoned."

Churchill then scrawled beneath the message and passed it back. It read, "NEVER FEAR. DEAD BIRDS DO NOT DROP OUT OF NESTS."

(I don't know about that. But I do know that at my age I am not going to risk . . .)

Platitudes—*Ineffectual*

In the 1930's, a Liberal Party statesman spoke at a London dinner on the League of Nations. The speaker soared to rhetorical heights as he depicted the day when there would be no war amid an era of international brotherhood. Afterward, a listener asked Churchill, who had attended the dinner, what he thought of the speech.

"WELL," he commented, "IT WAS GOOD. IT HAD TO BE GOOD, FOR IT CONTAINED ALL THE PLATITUDES KNOWN TO MAN, WITH THE POSSIBLE EXCEPTION OF 'PREPARE TO MEET THY GOD' AND 'PLEASE ADJUST YOUR TROUSERS BEFORE LEAVING.'"

(Well, when you strip out the generalities and platitudes of their policy statement . . .)

Media—*Equal Time*

In May 1955, a debate was conducted over the BBC entitled "Christianity vs. Atheism." When Churchill objected to the programming, the BBC spokesman responded. "It is our duty to truth to allow both sides to debate."

Churchill shot back, "I SUPPOSE THEN THAT IF THERE HAD BEEN THE SAME DEVICES AT THE TIME OF CHRIST, THE BBC WOULD HAVE GIVEN EQUAL TIME TO JUDAS AND JESUS."

(The media in their programming today seems to give more than a fair share of time to demagogues, self-appointed leaders, radical interest groups . . .)

Honoree—*Humanity*

During the wartime coalition, the president of the Board of Trade was the austere Calvinist, Sir Stafford Cripps. Cripps both tithed and teetotaled. He was even a vegetarian. His only concession to pleasure was smoking cigars, this habit too he swore off during the war, when he announced at a rally that he was now giving up cigars as a "salutary example of sacrifice."

Prime Minister Churchill, who was seated on the same platform, leaned over to a colleague and whispered, "TOO BAD—IT WAS HIS LAST CONTACT WITH HUMANITY."

(Our honoree tonight touches humanity in so many ways . . .)

Rules—*Results*

In 1941, Prime Minister Winston Churchill visited General Montgomery at the front. After a morning session of inspecting the troops, the Prime Minister offered a nip of whiskey. Monty refused, pounding his chest with the boast, "I neither drink nor smoke and I'm 100 percent fit."

Churchill put down his cigar and lifted his glass, replying, "I BOTH DRINK AND SMOKE AND I'M 200 PERCENT FIT."

(Well, I'm not so much interested in rules as in results. I don't care how you do it just so you *do* it!)

Investment—*Financing*

One weekend, while Churchill was resting at Chequers, the official country home of the British prime minister, the minister found Churchill retouching with his brush and oils Ruben's masterpiece of the ensnared lion being rescued by a mouse. Like a naughty boy caught in the act, Churchill looked sheepish. Then he muttered in defense, "I HAD TO

MAKE HIM BIGGER. HOW COULD SUCH A LITTLE MOUSE GNAW
OFF THE ROPES TO RESCUE THE BIG LION?"

(Similarly, our outlay for public relations and advertising
is too little to launch such major new moves . . .)

Planning—*Preparation*

In early 1945, President Roosevelt wrote to Churchill about
the agenda for the six-day conference of the Big Powers at
Yalta. F.D.R. felt there was no reason the plans for establish-
ing the U.N. could not be completed in the conference session. Churchill however, was doubtful. "I DON'T SEE ANY WAY
OF REALIZING OUR HOPES FOR A WORLD ORGANIZATION IN SIX
DAYS," he wrote F.D.R. "EVEN THE ALMIGHTY TOOK SEVEN."

(Before we launch such a major operation. We will need
a lot more time . . .)

Resolution—*Defiance*

After the deliverance at Dunkirk, Churchill rallied Britain
with his most memorable speech. "We shall fight on the
beaches, we shall fight on the landing grounds, we shall fight
in the fields and in the streets, we shall fight in the hills. We
shall never surrender."

Then, as the House of Commons thundered with cheers
at this stirring rhetoric, Churchill muttered in a whispered
aside to a colleague, "IF THEY DO LAND ON THE BEACHES,
WE'LL FIGHT THEM WITH THE BUTT ENDS OF BROKEN BEER
BOTTLES BECAUSE THAT'S BLOODY WELL ALL WE'VE GOT!"

Problem—*Rules*

At the Casablanca Conference in 1942, Churchill and Roosevelt met with Charles de Gaulle, the prickly leader of the
French Resistance. Churchill's chief aide, Brendan Bracken,
who was in charge of Churchill's arrangements, complained
of his boss' impossible demands.

Churchill replied, "Well, Brendan, you have only one cross to bear. I have a double cross—the double cross of Lorraine."

"The General's problem," sympathized Bracken, "is that he thinks he is the reincarnation of Joan of Arc."

"No, THE PROBLEM IS," concluded Churchill, "MY BISHOPS WON'T ALLOW ME TO BURN HIM."

(Similarly, what we'd like to do is not exactly what we *can* do.)

Speech—Audience

Once Churchill was sitting on an outside platform waiting to speak to crowds who had packed the streets to hear him. Beside him the chairlady of the proceedings leaned over and said, "Doesn't it thrill you, Mr. Churchill, to see all those people out there who came just to see you?"

Churchill replied, "IT IS QUITE FLATTERING, BUT WHEN-EVER I FEEL THIS WAY I ALWAYS REMEMBER THAT IF INSTEAD OF MAKING A POLITICAL SPEECH I WAS BEING HANGED, THE CROWD WOULD BE TWICE AS BIG."

Bureaucracy—Regulations

As a businessman, I am getting very frustrated with some of the nitpicking regulations the bureaucrats are writing in Washington. I recall the remarks of Churchill. During the wartime coalition, Churchill assigned to some Labourites a few of the more ceremonial but less meaningful ministries. One of these plums was given to Lord Privy Seal, whose responsibilities included the supervision of state papers. A particular document needed the signature of the prime minister, and the Lord Privy Seal dispatched his young aide to track down Churchill. Churchill was finally traced to the House of Commons lavatory, where clouds of billowing cigar smoke behind a stall door signaled his presence.

"Mr. Prime Minister," the aide said, rapping on the door, "the Lord Privy Seal requests your signature at once on a document important to the Crown."

Churchill, annoyed at being pestered by a man he thought he had carefully shelved, bellowed, "TELL THE LORD PRIVY SEAL THAT I AM SEALED IN MY 'PRIVY.'" Then he added, "AND I CAN ONLY DEAL WITH ONE SHIT AT A TIME."

(And today I plan to talk about just one new regulation . . .)

[Note: Only appropriate for selective audiences.]

Press—*Criticism*

When I think of what some of the newspapers have been writing, I think of Churchill's remarks. After a cross-country tour of the United States in the 1930s, the British parliamentarian was questioned in a Canadian press interview. "Mr. Churchill," a Canadian reporter asked, "do you have any criticism of America?"

Churchill thought and then replied, "THERE ARE ONLY TWO THINGS I DISLIKE ABOUT AMERICA. ITS TOILET PAPER IS TOO THIN AND ITS NEWSPAPERS TOO FAT."

(Churchill thought that newspapers were getting more like toilet paper. I might too, considering the crap we're reading . . .)

Criticism—*Misapplication*

Once when Winston Churchill was staying at the White House, Mrs. Roosevelt attacked him for his colonialist views on India. "The Indians," she charged, "have suffered years under British oppression."

Churchill replied: "WELL, MRS. R., ARE WE TALKING ABOUT THE BROWN-SKINNED INDIANS IN INDIA WHO HAVE MULTIPLIED ALARMINGLY UNDER BENEVOLENT BRITISH RULE, OR ARE WE SPEAKING ABOUT THE RED-SKINNED INDIANS IN AMERICA WHO, I UNDERSTAND, ARE NOW EXTINCT?"

(Churchill was expressing the old axiom that people in glass houses should not throw stones.)

Business—Initiative

In my opinion, anyone who is anti-business is anti-jobs, anti-growth and anti-America. I recall what Churchill said to the Socialist who was touting the virtues of an economy regulated by government. As an example, the Socialist cited the increase in general population under the previous three years of the Labourites' administration. Churchill's ears pricked up as he heard the figure and rose to ask the speaker a question.

"WOULDN'T THE HONOURABLE GENTLEMAN CONCEDE THAT THE LAST STATISTIC ABOUT POPULATION IS DUE NOT TO SOCIALISM BUT RATHER TO PRIVATE ENTERPRISE?"

Toast—Opening

As I offer a toast to the beginning of this endeavor, I recall the words of Winston Churchill. He was First Lord of the Admiralty in the First World War and was approached by the head of the women's temperance union to reconsider the Royal Navy's practice of christening a ship by breaking a bottle of champagne across its bow.

"BUT MADAME CHAIRMAN," replied Churchill, "THE HALLOWED CUSTOM OF THE ROYAL NAVY IS INDEED A SPLENDID EXAMPLE OF TEMPERANCE. THE SHIP TAKES ITS FIRST SIP OF WINE AND THEN HAPPILY PROCEEDS ON WATER EVER AFTER."

Age—Birthday

On his seventy-fifth birthday, a reporter encountered Churchill as he left his London Hyde Park residence and asked, "Mr. Churchill, do you have any fear of death?"

"I AM READY TO MEET MY MAKER," Churchill replied, and

then he added with a twinkle, "BUT WHETHER MY MAKER IS PREPARED FOR THE GREAT ORDEAL OF MEETING ME IS ANOTHER MATTER."

Family—*Priority*

I'm a great admirer of Churchill, except perhaps in one area. I'm referring to the time when Sir Winston took a cruise on an Italian ship. A journalist from a Rome newspaper cornered the former prime minister to ask him why he chose to travel on an Italian line when the stately Queen's line under the British flag was available. Churchill gave the question his consideration and then gravely replied, "THERE ARE THREE THINGS I LIKE ABOUT ITALIAN SHIPS. FIRST, THEIR CUISINE, WHICH IS UNSURPASSED. SECOND, THEIR SERVICE, WHICH IS QUITE SUPERB." And then Sir Winston added, "AND THEN, IN TIME OF EMERGENCY, THERE IS NONE OF THIS NONSENSE ABOUT WOMEN AND CHILDREN FIRST."

(But seriously, the needs of the family must come first.)

Family—*In-laws*

The subject of in-laws reminds me of an experience Winston Churchill had. Churchill's oldest daughter, Sarah, had married Vic Oliver, a music-hall comedian. At a family dinner, Oliver, who brought along a guest, tried to draw out his famous father-in-law from one of his periodic silent moods. "Winston, who, in your opinion, was the greatest statesman you have ever known?"

"Benito Mussolini," was the unexpected reply.

"What? Why is that?" said a surprised Oliver.

"MUSSOLINI IS THE ONLY STATESMAN," grumbled Churchill, "WHO HAD THE REQUISITE COURAGE TO HAVE HIS OWN SON-IN-LAW EXECUTED."

(Of course, some of us know Count Ciano, the former Italian Foreign Secretary who married Mussolini's daughter and was shot in 1942. But unlike Churchill, I have much affection for my son-in-law.)

Wife—*Toast*

As I begin this toast, I think of something Winston Churchill once said. He was at a formal banquet in London, where the attending dignitaries were asked the question, "If you could not be who you are, who would you like to be?" Naturally everyone was curious as to what Churchill would say. Napolean? Julius Caesar? Alexander the Great? When it finally came Churchill's turn, the old man, who was the dinner's last respondent, rose and gave his answer.

"IF I COULD NOT BE WHO I AM, I WOULD MOST LIKE TO BE"—and here he paused to take his wife's hand—"LADY CHURCHILL'S SECOND HUSBAND."

Age—*Retirement*

I know that with my advancing years there has been some talk that I should step down. I would like to be able to say what Churchill once said.

When Winston Churchill returned to 10 Downing Street for the second time in 1951, there was some criticism about his advanced age. A year later, a reporter cornered the seventy-eight-year-old prime minister and asked him if he was going to make his announcement to retire soon. Churchill growled, "NOT UNTIL I'M A GREAT DEAL WORSE AND THE EMPIRE A GREAT DEAL BETTER."

Weariness—*Banalities*

During a long session in the House of Commons, one of Churchill's opponents was droning on in a long speech. Churchill slumped in his seat and closed his eyes. The speaker said, "Must the right honorable gentleman fall asleep when I am speaking?"

Churchill blithely replied, "NO, IT IS PURELY VOLUNTARY."

Accident—*Correct*

When I hear what the Senator is saying, I think of the Socialist who once interrupted a Churchill speech with a rebutting fact. Churchill shrugged it off, saying, "I DO NOT CHALLENGE THE HONOURABLE GENTLEMAN WHEN THE TRUTH LEAKS OUT OF HIM BY ACCIDENT FROM TIME TO TIME."

(Well, as a staunch Republican, I find myself agreeing with the Democratic candidate on his views about . . .)

Speech—*Inadequacy*

As I begin my talk, I think of Churchill's comment to an inexperienced speaker after he had delivered an address that was haltingly tedious. Churchill said, with mock sympathy:

"I CAN WELL UNDERSTAND THE HONORABLE MEMBER'S WISHING TO SPEAK FOR PRACTICE. HE NEEDS IT BADLY."

(I'm afraid that if Churchill were here today he would say the same thing of me . . .)

Memorable—*Occasion*

Winston Churchill was accosted by a member of the audience after a talk. The man grabbed Churchill's sleeve and said, "Mr. Churchill, perhaps you don't remember me, but I was the pubkeeper at the King's Arms when you were the Member from Dundee before the Great War. But you might recall Molly, a buxom lass of fair face and full figure who was the barmaid at the King's Arms."

"NO DOUBT I WOULD HAVE REMEMBERED IF I HAD BEEN IN MOLLY'S ARMS."

(No one could forget the occasion we are celebrating tonight.)

Morale—*Toast*

In the manner of Winston Churchill, I would like to pay trib-
ute to the splendid spirit of this organization. In 1951, when
Churchill returned to Number 10 Downing Street, the first
trip he took away from Britain was to France, to meet with
General Eisenhower, the newly appointed head of the Allied
N.A.T.O. command. At his chateau outside Paris, General
Eisenhower entertained his old friend at a luncheon. During
the luncheon Eisenhower spoke earnestly of the need for
more forces. He continued well after the dessert. At one point
Churchill, noticing an ornate credenza behind Eisenhower on
which a decanter of brandy stood, said, "Dwight, that's a
handsome credenza. Is it Louis Seize?" (the Sixteenth)

Eisenhower despite a nudge from his deputy, General Al
Gruenther, said, "I guess it is—it was here when I came."
and Ike went on speaking about the enlargement of the
British contingent.

Then Churchill interjected, "And that's a splendid
decanter on the credenza. Is it Austrian crystal?"

Ike replied, "I suppose, but about this manpower
problem . . ."

To which Churchill said, "MORE THAN MANPOWER, IT'S
MORALE—AND THE FIRST THING THE SUPREME ALLIED COM-
MANDER MUST DO IS LIFT THE 'SPIRITS' ON THAT CREDENZA."

Political Correctness—*Stupidity*

Some of us get sick of the language of political correctness.
We feel like Churchill who was getting quite restless and
bored as a Socialist academic delivered his tirade against big
business and the rich.

Churchill commented, "VERBOSITY MAY BE THE LONG
SUIT OF THE HONOURABLE GENTLEMAN, BUT IT'S NOT LONG
ENOUGH TO COVER HIS ASS-INITY."

(Well, the dressing up of high-sounding words is not enough to hide the foolishness of this proposal.)

Criticism—*Anonymity*

The worst kind of criticism is cowardly criticism from critics who won't show their faces or give their names. I remember once when Churchill was about to begin his stump speech in one of his campaigns and a party officer handed him a large envelope. Churchill assumed it was some sort of notice and held up his hand for silence. He opened the envelope and took out a sheet of paper. The word "fool" was written on it.

Churchill looked at his attentive audience and said, "This is most unusual. I have just been handed a message which consists of but one word—the word 'fool.' I repeat this is most unusual. I HAVE OFTEN HEARD OF THOSE WHO HAVE WRITTEN LETTERS AND FORGOTTEN TO SIGN THEIR NAMES, BUT THIS IS THE FIRST TIME I HAVE EVER HEARD OF ANYONE WHO SIGNED HIS NAME AND FORGOT TO WRITE THE LETTER."

Support—*Involvement*

One Easter Sunday Winston Churchill made an appearance at the parish church near his home at Chartwell. After the service, the rector, noting the infrequency of his visits, said, "Well, Prime Minister, you are not quite a pillar of the church, are you?"

"No," said Churchill, "I'M A BUTTRESS—I SUPPORT IT FROM THE OUTSIDE."

(Well, today we salute one who—though he is not one of us—has supported . . .)

Concentration—*Objective*

Churchill, among his many pursuits, raised horses. In 1949, his black stallion Colonist was a favorite at the Derby. Just before the race Churchill went into the stables and tried to exhort his steed to victory, just as he had rallied his nation during the war.

Stroking his horse on the backside, he orated his call to action, ending with this promise:

"If you win today, Colonist, I pledge to you, it will be your last race. Think of it—the rest of your life in stud. Just imagine those verdant pastures replete with lissome, nubile fillies, waiting to attend to all of your needs."

Alas, Colonist finished far out of the running. When Churchill was asked what happened, he replied, "POOR COLONIST, WHEN I SAID WHAT WAS AWAITING HIM, HE COULDN'T KEEP HIS MIND ON THE RACE."

(We must not lose sight of our principal objective . . .)

Urgency—*Time*

In 1951, the Prime Minister, while visiting Washington, was taken for a cruise on the Williamsburg yacht down the Potomac. In the high-ceilinged salon, while Churchill was sipping his brandy, he turned to his scientific aide Lord Cherwell, a former mathematics professor.

"Prof," he asked, "if all the wine, whiskey, and spirits that I have drunk were to be poured in this salon, would it fill it to the ceiling?"

Cherwell took out his slide-rule and made his calculations.

"Unfortunately, Prime Minister, if all the alcohol you have consumed were to occupy this salon, it would only rise to your eye-level."

Churchill replied, "As I contemplate my 77 years and look at the ceiling, my only thought is, HOW MUCH LEFT TO DO AND HOW LITTLE TIME TO DO IT!"

(Well, similarly, time is running out . . .)

Proposal—*Mistake*

A newly elected member of Parliament asked the great man about the speech he had just delivered.

"Mr. Churchill, how could I have put more fire in it?"

"YOUR PROBLEM," said Churchill, "IS NOT MORE FIRE IN THE SPEECH BUT THAT YOU DIDN'T PUT THAT SPEECH IN THE FIRE!"

(Well, similarly, the proposal cannot be improved by small changes because it is a bad plan from the outset.)

Introduction—*Brevity*

Churchill founded before the First World War "The Other Club." The purpose was to encourage spirited argument and raucous bantering.

One custom was to call on a member to give a short address on a topic that was sprung on him at the last moment.

Once Churchill's name was called and he was told his subject was "*Sex.*"

Churchill rose and intoned in his stately growl, "SEX—IT GIVES ME GREAT PLEASURE . . . " and then sat down.

(Well, I will be brief in saying what pleasure it gives me to introduce . . .)

Excellence—*Best*

After World War II Churchill came to America on one of his speaking tours. The Plaza Hotel in New York, where he was going to stay on one of his lectures, tried to learn Mr. Churchill's tastes.

The manager called the British embassy in Washington and inquired.

"I'm calling from the Plaza Hotel in New York to ask about Mr. Churchill's preferences."

Immediately the call was switched and a lisped growl barked, "Yes?"

"I am calling to ascertain Mr. Churchill's tastes . . . "

The voice answered, "MR. CHURCHILL IS A MAN OF SIM-PLE TASTES—EASILY SATISFIED WITH THE BEST."

(Well, we too are simple in our request—nothing less than the best.)

Bureaucracy—*Communication*

When Churchill headed the Conservative Party in Opposition after the war, he fought the Socialist administration. Just as bad as their policies was their jargon. The poor were called "marginal stipend maintainers," a cap on wages, "incremental arrests." The worst was their calling a house or home a "local accommodation unit."

Churchill said in a speech:

"I SUPPOSE NOW WE WILL HAVE TO CHANGE THAT OLD AND FAVORITE SONG 'HOME, SWEET HOME' TO 'LOCAL ACCOMMO-DATION UNIT, SWEET LOCAL ACCOMMODATION UNIT'!"

(Well, cannot we pierce through the jargon of this report and say in a few simple words . . .)

Defeat—*Dismissal*

When Churchill was defeated in 1945, King George VI wanted to award him Knight of the Garter.

He replied, "WHY SHOULD I ACCEPT FROM MY SOVEREIGN THE ORDER OF THE GARTER WHEN HIS PEOPLE HAVE ALREADY GIVEN ME THE 'ORDER OF THE BOOT'?"

(Well, I have similarly received . . .)

ASSEMBLY HALL

I have never let my schooling interfere with my education.

Mark Twain

Schoolmasters and parents exist to be grown out of.

Sir John Wolfenden

He who can does. He who cannot teaches.

George Bernard Shaw

When a teacher calls a boy by his entire name, it means trouble.

Mark Twain

Expensive—*Spending*

Because of economic conditions, a famous New England prep school was obliged to raise its tuition. A letter informed parents of this fact, stating that there would be an increase of $5,000 per annum. Unfortunately, in the letter, it was spelled "per anum." An angry parent wrote to the headmaster of the school thanking him for the notification and saying, "FOR MY PART I WOULD PREFER TO CONTINUE PAYING THROUGH THE NOSE."

(Well, I say it is asinine to continue to pay through the nose for . . .)

Mixup—*Communication*

Sometimes the left hand doesn't know what the right hand is doing and one department can get in trouble because it doesn't know what the other department is saying.

Some years ago, an Episcopal bishop was invited to talk to the student body of a well-known prep school in Massachusetts. "What subject would you like me to talk about?" asked the bishop. The headmaster replied, "It would be very helpful if you'd give them a talk about sex."

After a little hesitation, the clergyman accepted. But when he got home, he didn't quite dare tell his wife the subject he had been given, so he told a white lie: "I was asked to talk on sailing." His wife seemed puzzled, but the conversation moved on to other things.

A few days later, a school parent remarked to the bishop's wife, "Your husband gave a wonderful talk to the student body."

"I'M AMAZED," said the wife. "HE'S ONLY DONE IT THREE TIMES. THE FIRST TIME HE GOT SICK TO HIS STOMACH. THE SECOND TIME HIS HAT BLEW OFF. AND THE THIRD TIME HIS FOOT GOT CAUGHT IN THE TOP SHEET."

Promises—*Spending*

I remember hearing about "sharing time" in a kindergarten full of bright children. The teacher was presiding over a discussion about the children's fathers and mothers. One child said, "Well, my mother's a Catholic and my father's a Jew."

"Oh, wow!" said another. "So what do you believe?"

"I believe in everything!" said the first child.

"What do you mean, everything?" asked another child.

"YOU KNOW," said the first child, "SANTA CLAUS, HANUKKAH, THE TOOTH FAIRY, THE EASTER BUNNY, ANYTHING ELSE THAT OFFERS GOODIES AND TOYS."

(A lot of people out there will believe in anybody or anything that offers a free lunch.)

Repeat—*Bottom Line*

A neighbor told me about one time when she asked her daughter in the first grade what she had learned in school that day. "Rithmatick," the daughter proudly said. "We learned addition: four plus four, the son-of-a-bitch is eight, eight plus eight, the son-of-a-bitch is sixteen."

"Judy!" shouted her mother. "Watch your language! You're not allowed to use swear-words like *son-of-a-bitch*."

"But, Mom," replied Judy, "that's what the teacher taught us, and she said to recite it out loud till we learned it all."

Next day Judy's mother went to school with her daughter and marched right into the classroom to complain. "Oh, heavens!" said the teacher. "That's not what I taught them. They're supposed to say, 'TWO PLUS TWO, THE SUM OF WHICH IS FOUR.'"

(Well, today we are doing some 'rithmatick'—the 'sum of which,' are some bottom line totals.)

Surveys—*Research*

I remember hearing a story from my child's school.

The teacher called on a boy, who was looking out the window and didn't respond at all. So the teacher said, quite loudly and sharply, "What is your opinion of the question we're discussing?"

"Oh, I'm sorry, sir, I didn't hear you," said the boy. "I was lost in thought."

"WELL," said the teacher, "I'M NOT SURPRISED YOU WERE LOST. I REALIZE IT'S UNFAMILIAR TERRITORY."

(Similarly, unless we do the proper research, we will be in unfamiliar territory, not knowing the direction in which we are heading.)

Mess—*Incredible*

I know all of you have an idea from the newspaper of just how critical conditions are. But I want to say that the situation is even worse than what you have read. It is like something my nephew said not long ago.

Now, it is the custom in our family to ask at Sunday dinner what the children had learned in Sunday School. So, one day I asked my nephew who was visiting what the lesson had been that day, and he said it was Moses and the fleeing Israelites.

"What did you find out about them?" I asked.

"Well," said the boy, "there were these Israelites and they were trying to escape from the bad Egyptians and the Egyptians chased them right to the Red Sea."

"Yes, and then what happened?"

"Well, Moses took out his walkie-talkie and said, 'Chief Engineer, build the pontoon.' And then over the pontoon the Israelites went."

"Well, the Egyptians started to come over the pontoon, too, and so Moses picked up the walkie-talkie again and said, 'Chief Engineer, dynamite the pontoon,' and the Egyptians went down in the ocean."

And I said: "Are you sure that's how the teacher told it to you?"

"WELL, NOT EXACTLY. BUT IF I TOLD IT TO YOU THE WAY SHE TOLD IT TO ME, YOU'D NEVER BELIEVE IT!"

(And you're going to have a hard time believing about the operation . . .)

Communication—*Interpretation*

Sometimes we don't convey our message because the audience chooses to hear only what they want to hear. For example, one time a schoolteacher was lecturing to the third grade the dangers of not bundling up properly to face the winter cold.

"The son of my neighbor—an only child—disobeyed his mother and went out sledding one afternoon without his cap, mittens and snow suit. Because of it, he caught pneumonia and died."

Afterwards, one boy raised his hand.

"Yes, Johnny," the teacher replied.

"Miss Thatcher, may I ask you two questions?"

"Go ahead, Johnny."

"WHO HAS HIS SLED NOW AND COULD I HAVE IT?"

Generalities—*Specifics*

The story is told about that eminent doctor whose name is a household word with all young mothers as the ultimate authority on child rearing.

One Saturday afternoon he was paving the driveway in front of his Boston garage. All of a sudden some neighborhood boys raced across the wet cement, leaving their footprints. The venerable doctor let loose a spate of Anglo-Saxon monosyllabics not found in a dictionary. His wife remonstrated, "Dear, what would your fans think of your reputed compassion for children?"

"DEAR," he replied, "I LOVE CHILDREN IN THE ABSTRACT—BUT NOT IN THE CONCRETE."

(Well, we all agree in the abstract on the general tenor of the proposal; it is some of the concrete specifics we have problem with . . .)

Rating—*Conduct*

When we have to rate the performances of others, sometimes we bend over backwards to be tactful. For example, schoolteachers and principals often feel that they must try to say something favorable about students who really aren't doing that well. Thus, one principal wrote on a report card, "This boy, I fear, does his best."

And a grade adviser, required to write a reference for a younger student in connection with a summer job, wrote, "Conduct generally good." The prospective employer called up to ask for more specifics. "What do you mean, 'generally?'" he asked.

"Oh," said the grade adviser, "NOT PARTICULARLY."

(In contrast, the one we honor tonight has been *particularly* singled out for this challenge . . .)

Credibility

I remember what a wise teacher said to a family in my neighborhood. At the end of the term she sent a note: "IF YOU PROMISE NOT TO BELIEVE EVERYTHING YOUR CHILD SAYS HAPPENS AT SCHOOL, I PROMISE NOT TO BELIEVE EVERYTHING HE SAYS HAPPENS AT HOME."

BARRACKS AND BATTLESHIPS

The best service a retired general can perform is turn in his tongue along with his suit.

> Gen. Omar Bradley

If it moves, salute it; if it doesn't move, pick it up; if you can't pick it up, paint it.

> Army saying

War is too important a matter to be left to the generals.

> Georges Clemenceau

The main object of the army is to promote the generals' welfare.

> From the Humes File

Return—Style

During World War II, the Eisenhowers made their home in the old Wardman Park Hotel. Most of the time General Eisenhower was away—first in North Africa and then in England. But he regularly returned to report to Washington.

Because of wartime restrictions his wife Mamie never knew when he would arrive, so she kept a day bed in the living room, which could be pulled out when he arrived back in Washington in the wee hours of the morning.

Mamie Eisenhower, in telling of the experience, would say, "Sometimes I'd awake from sleep and go to the bathroom—AND WHEN I SAW THE SEAT WAS UP, I'D CRY BECAUSE I KNEW THEN MY IKE WAS HOME."

(Well, every executive puts his or her own stamp on the way daily functions are carried out . . .)

Marketing—*Consumer Strategy*

What we should ask ourselves is, who is it we want to reach? I recall the answer a young Marine gave to a nurse while recovering at a Navy hospital. The youthful leatherneck was composing a letter back home to his wife. A kind-hearted nurse was taking down the note.

"The nurses here," he dictated, "are a rather plain lot."

"Why," exclaimed the nurse, "don't you think that's rather unfair?"

The soldier smiled and replied, "YES, BUT IT WILL MAKE MY WIFE VERY HAPPY."

Plans—*Expert*

I find myself in agreement with the proposition, if a little uncertain on the general details of execution. In that way I am not unlike George Washington who, as a member of Virginia's House of Burgesses in 1775, met secretly to discuss the worsening situation with Britain.

At Williamsburg's Raleigh Tavern the dissident colonials talked strategy. Young Tom Jefferson said, "As for me, there is no country in the world I would rather be dependent on than Britain, but if the Tory government continues to deny us our rights, I would move body and soul to sink that island to the bottom of the Atlantic Ocean."

Colonel Washington replied, "The sentiments of Mr. Jefferson are also mine. It is the time to move for independence. But as a military man, I must say, as to Mr. Jefferson's specific plan of routing the British, I WILL LEAVE THAT TO THE NAVAL EXPERTS."

(And so while I generally approve of the project, I would like to consult other experts . . .)

Conviction—*Popularity*

Having the courage to do the right thing and persisting in your course does not win friends from among your critics, if you prove them wrong. This was especially true when the Congress of Vienna was held to settle the map of Europe after the Napoleonic wars. It was attended by all the European nations, even the defeated French. The Duke of Wellington, conqueror of Napoleon at the Battle of Waterloo, was there as the ambassador from Britain.

Some French officers, unwilling to greet the conqueror, turned their backs on him in disdain. When King Louis apologized to the English general, Wellington shrugged and said, "IT DOES NOT MATTER, I HAVE SEEN THE BACKS OF FRENCH OFFICERS BEFORE."

(Well, leadership is a matter of courage and conviction and real leaders are not always popular.)

Language—*Communication*

Some experts blame the schools. Others blame television. But the fact is that the ability to express oneself is a shrinking commodity. An English professor of mine who had served in World War II told us about the time a shipboard mate took a shore leave in Pearl Harbor.

The sailor was telling the future professor what he had done on his overnight leave from the base. He said, "I left that f— base, and waited around for a f— hour or so for the f— bus. Finally, it came, and we rode to the f— town. I went into this f— bar, and there was this f— doll, so I ordered her a f— drink. Well, by now we were getting pretty f— friendly. We left the f— bar and walked down the f— main street till I saw a f— little hotel, and we went in. I paid and we went up the f— stairs and into this f— little room."

"Really?" said his more academically inclined shipmate. "And what did you do then?"

"What do you think?" said the sailor. "WE HAD SEXUAL INTERCOURSE."

(The English language has more words than French and German combined. You would think that might help us to communicate more clearly.)

[Note: As a teacher this is a favorite story of mine, but it obviously can only be used with selected audiences.]

Solution—*Stopgap*

Too many times we look for the easy fix, the stop-gap solution. We are not unlike the soldier from Fort Knox who, with his girlfriend, hurried into a judge's office in my county one afternoon and asked the judge to marry them.

"Got a license?" the judge asked.

"No, Judge," said the would-be bride. "John just got out for weekend leave and the clerk's office is already closed."

"Sorry," said the judge, "I can't do it. Come back on Monday and we'll have the ceremony."

"But Judge," pleaded the girl, "John is just here for two days. He is being shipped overseas at 8:00 A.M. Monday morning."

"I'm sorry, I can't help you," said the judge. "I can't marry you without a license."

"BUT JUDGE," said the not-to-be downed soldier, "COULDN'T YOU SAY JUST A FEW WORDS TO TIDE US OVER THE WEEKEND?"

(Today, we are not looking for the temporary solution but for a long-range plan.)

Homework—*Preparation*

Many on the West Point football team sign up for Spanish as their obligatory language requirement—much to the exasperation of a certain romance languages professor.

On one exam, this particular Spanish professor asked his students, "Who was Sancho Panza?"

One big lineman wrote in his blue exam book, "Sancho Panza was a little fat guy who rode around on a *burrow*."

The professor flunked him, saying, "'Burro' (B-U-R-R-O) is a donkey or an ass. 'Burrow' (B-U-R-R-O-W) is a hole in the ground." And then he added, "AND SO, AS A FUTURE OFFICER AND GENTLEMEN IT'S TIME YOU KNEW ONE FROM THE OTHER."

(Well, those of you who think you can get by without the proper preparation will never become top executives.)

Planning—*Flexibility*

In 1787, General George Washington presided over the convention that wrote the U.S. Constitution. He spoke little during this historic meeting, except when the provision of a standing army was debated. The convention added a provision that the army would be limited to 3,000 men and Washington could be quiet no longer. "IF THAT IS SO," he said, "LET THE CONSTITUTION ALSO SAY THAT NO FOREIGN ARMY SHOULD EVER INVADE OUR COUNTRY WITH MORE THAN 3,000 TROOPS."

(Like George Washington we must take into account all future contingencies and possible problems.)

Prospect—*Problems*

At a splendid white tie dinner at the Guild Hall in London a few years ago, held to honor the victory of the Battle of Britain, a mustached major general of the R.A.F sat at the head table with the Victoria Cross hanging on a gold ribbon around his neck. Next to him sat the wife of the Lord Mayor of London, who sported a rose in the valley of her decolletage.

At one point the general leaned over as if to pluck the rose of the Lady Mayoress, saying, "Madam, if I pulled this rose, would it make you blush?"

The lady reacted by putting her finger on the gold ribbon around the general's neck, saying, "GENERAL, IF I PULLED THIS CHAIN, WOULD IT MAKE YOU FLUSH?"

(So you see, as attractive a possibility as the opportunity may seem, we have to consider some of our own liabilities . . .)

Mistake—*Next Time*

Next time, gentlemen, I assure you I won't make the same mistake. All you need is one lesson like that of a certain French aide-de-camp. After his heroics in France in World War I, the legendary Sergeant York was decorated by the President of France. At a reception later he was approached by a pretty French girl who said, "Sergeant, did you really kill a German soldier in battle?"

"Yup."

"With what hand did you do it?" asked the girl.

"With this right hand, Ma'mselle," replied York.

At that point the coquettish French girl seized his right hand and kissed it.

A French colonel beside York said, "GOOD HEAVENS,

YORK. NEXT TIME WHY DON'T YOU TELL A GIRL THAT YOU BIT
THE GERMAN TO DEATH?"

(Well, if we could do it over again . . .)

Expensive—*Temporary*

As we consider the cost of such an undertaking, it might be
wise to recall the story of General Douglas MacArthur. The
former general in his last years instructed an aide to pur-
chase a monument or burial crypt suitable to the majesty of
the general. After much study the aide brought back a plan
for a magnificent mausoleum in Norfolk, Virginia.
MacArthur studied it, then rejected it. "Impossible—much
too costly." The aide went back to the architects. After some
months the aide was shown a plan for an elegant obelisk. He
brought it to the attention of the general. Again MacArthur
objected to the expense. So the aide consulted the architects
once more and another plan was presented. This design
showed a simple tall memorial shaft with a place for
entombment. MacArthur was apparently satisfied until he
asked the aide for the price.

"General, it will be two hundred thousand dollars."

"ISN'T THAT A BIT EXPENSIVE? I ONLY NEED IT FOR THREE
DAYS."

(And similarly, I would say it is much too expensive for a
project that . . .)

Press—*Misreporting*

On his ship's leave, the first mate got so drunk that he didn't
show for his duties. It was not until the second day out at sea
that, rather the worse for wear, he managed to stand watch.

To his horror, however, he noted in the ship's log the
damning statement: "Unfortunately, First Mate Johnson was
drunk all day."

He sought out the captain at the first opportunity. "Captain," he said, "this is the first time in my years of service that I have ever been too drunk to serve. Please remove the notation."

The captain scowled. "You know the log can't be changed."

The first mate said, "But with that on my record, I may have trouble ever getting a captain's berth of my own."

"I can't help that," said the captain remorselessly. "The statement is perfectly true, and that is the only thing we should be concerned with."

Whereupon the first mate returned to his duties and entered a notation of his own in the log: "FORTUNATELY, CAPTAIN SIMPSON WAS SOBER ALL DAY."

(Similarly, the press has been very selective with its facts and what they said was out of context.)

Appeasement—*Negotiation*

In his dealings with Adolf Hitler, British Prime Minister Neville Chamberlain seemed to think that saving a millon lives was well worth the surrender of England's honor. His conferences with Hitler at Berchtesgaden and Godesberg read like the diary of a young lady crossing the Atlantic for the first time.

Monday—I feel highly honored at being placed at the Captain's table.

Tuesday—I spent the morning on the bridge with the Captain. He seemed to like me.

Wednesday—The Captain made proposals to me unbecoming an officer and a gentleman.

Thursday—The Captain threatened to sink the ship unless I agreed to his proposals.

Friday—I SAVED SIX HUNDRED LIVES!

(Well, the surrendering of principle—however tempting—is a recipe for disaster.)

BENCH AND BAR

A judge is a law student who marks his own examination papers.

H.L. Mencken

A jury consists of twelve persons chosen to decide who has the better lawyer.

Robert Frost

The best way to get a bad law repealed is to enforce it strictly.

Abraham Lincoln

God works wonders, now and then. Behold! A lawyer and an honest man.

Benjamin Franklin

I used to be a lawyer but now I am a reformed character.

Woodrow Wilson

When both judge and jury are against a man, thirteen is an unlucky number.

From the Humes File

Conversion—*Change of Mind*

Sometimes the facts persuade us to change our minds. I remember a case in Philadelphia, where a woman summoned for jury duty said to the Judge, "Your Honor, I can't serve on a jury. I don't believe in capital punishment."

"Madam," replied the Judge patiently, "this isn't a capital charge so that doesn't matter. This is a case where a husband emptied out the wife's savings account of $14,000 to take a three-day weekend with his girlfriend in Atlantic City."

"JUDGE," she replied, "I'LL SERVE. I COULD BE WRONG ABOUT CAPITAL PUNISHMENT."

Good News—*Bad News*

Moses must have been the first lawyer because he came down from the mountain and told his people, "Brethren, I have good news and bad news. The good news is that I argued Him down to Ten. THE BAD NEWS IS ADULTERY STAYS IN."

Purpose—*Direction*

Justice Oliver Wendell Holmes once boarded a train in Washington then promptly lost his ticket. The conductor recognized him and said, "Never mind, Mr. Justice. When you find your ticket I am certain you will mail it in."

"Mr. Conductor," replied Holmes, "the question is not, 'Where is my ticket?' but, 'WHERE AM I SUPPOSED TO BE GOING?'"

(Well, first we have to determine what our purpose is and where we are heading . . .)

Justice—*Change*

It is with some apprehension that I admit a great respect for lawyers of this bar; in particular for their astuteness and skill. I recall some years ago a senior partner of a very prestigious law firm in this city was representing the defense against a plaintiff—an old lady who was suing an airline for injuries she suffered coming off the airplane platform steps. But the trial dragged on into the judge's scheduled vacation in Miami, so he turned the case over to a junior associate. One day, when he got back from the beach, the hotel clerk handed him a telegram. It was from his associate and it read, "Justice has prevailed."

Somewhat distressed, the judge immediately called

Western Union and sent a wire to his junior associate. It read, "APPEAL AT ONCE."

(We are happy to say that justice has prevailed in this situation and we see no cause for . . .)

Reverse—*Role*

In 1804, there occurred in American history the only impeachment trial of a U.S. Supreme Court Justice.

After the House of Representatives voted to impeach Justice Samuel Chase he was tried for judicial misconduct. The trial was held in the Senate and was presided over by Vice President Burr, who had recently killed Alexander Hamilton in a duel.

Congressman John Randolph of Virginia was asked what he thought of the trial. "A bit odd," he replied. "Usually a murderer is arraigned before the judge. HERE A JUDGE IS ARRAIGNED BEFORE A MURDERER!"

(Well, I find myself today playing the reverse of my usual role tonight . . .)

Appreciation—*Client*

Clarence Darrow, the lawyer who built a reputation for defending highly unpopular causes, almost never asked about a client's ability to pay before deciding to take a case. As a result he often found that his clients *had* no way of paying him for his legal services. After one of his cases had come to a happy conclusion, his client said to him. "Mr. Darrow, how can I ever express my appreciation?"

Darrow answered, "EVER SINCE THE PHOENICIANS INVENTED MONEY, THERE HAS BEEN ONLY ONE WAY TO SAY THANK YOU."

(If you are grateful for our services, I hope you will repay us by giving us more business.)

Litigiousness—*Lawyers*

When we consider the possible legal liability, I am reminded of the young law school graduate at the Bar Association dinner. He had just passed the bar and was asked to say a prayer. Unprepared, and preoccupied with his own prospects, he blurted out, "OH, LORD, STIR UP MUCH STRIFE AMONGST THY PEOPLE LEST I, THY HUMBLE SERVANT, PERISH . . . "

Consistency—*Facts*

I have heard the criticism and am reminded of the time when the prize witness for the defense was called to the stand. She paid no attention to the swearing-in procedure. "Young lady," asked the judge sternly, "are you fully aware of the implications of the oath you have just taken?"

Snapping her gum, the woman replied, "YEAH, SURE. IT MEANS IF I TELL A LIE, I GOTTA STICK TO IT."

(Well, we have told the truth and we will stick to our position.)

Congratulations—*Mixed Feelings*

The paternity case involving a well-known New York baseball player was in all the gossip columns for weeks, and the Florida judge's decision was eagerly awaited. On the appointed day, the magistrate emerged from his chambers with a suitably solemn expression. His black robe trailing impressively behind him, he ascended the steps to the bench and looked down gravely on the sea of faces awaiting his decision. Finally the judge took a deep breath, withdrew a cigar from the recesses of his robe, and handed it to the defendant with a flourish.

"CONGRATULATIONS," he pronounced solemnly. "YOU HAVE JUST BECOME A FATHER."

(Though not in the same way, I have some mixed feelings about the congratulations being extended me.)

Ethics—*Problem*

An ancient, nearly blind woman retained the local lawyer to draft her last will and testament, for which he charged her two hundred dollars. As she rose to leave, she took the money out of her purse and handed it over, enclosing a third hundred-dollar bill by mistake. Immediately the attorney realized he faced a crushing ethical question:

SHOULD HE TELL HIS PARTNER?

Arrangements—*Change*

The young lawyer decided to take the plunge and go into practice for himself, but times were tough and pickings slim. So he was delighted when an ancient spinster walked into his office and asked him to draft her will. "I've got twelve thousand dollars," she informed him, "and when I die I want the fanciest funeral this hick town has ever seen: the couturier gown, solid mahogany coffin, orchids flown in from Brazil, and a full choir singing Bach cantatas. I've checked prices and all this'll cost about ten thousand dollars. That leaves me two grand. Now I don't want to go to my grave a virgin, and I figure that for that price, some young man will be willing to go to bed with me."

The lawyer's eyes widened. Later after he'd reported the conversation to his wife and they'd discussed all the ways in which the income would come in handy, she agreed to drop him off at the old woman's house that evening. "Pick me up in two hours, honey," he instructed.

Two hours later his wife pulled back into the old woman's driveway and tooted the car horn. The lawyer stuck his head out of an upstairs window and yelled down, "COME BACK ON SUNDAY—SHE'S DECIDED TO LET THE COUNTY BURY HER!"

(Well, sometimes arrangements have to be changed . . .)

General Counsel—*Attorney*

Years ago, in New York, I knew a lawyer who was a fanatical fly fisherman. Each vacation he spent in search of the perfect trout stream. He finally came across an idyllic spot in the Allegheny foothills of upstate Pennsylvania—a place called Trout Run. One of its attractions being the sweet young thing who worked at the rundown motel down the highway. Each year the big city attorney returned in pursuit of both the fish and the girl, and he finally had his way with her.

When his Cadillac pulled up in front of the motel the next year, he was flabbergasted. There behind the desk sat the sweet young thing—with a baby on her lap. "Why, honey, why didn't you tell me?" he stammered. "Why, I would have done right by you, fetched you and married you . . ."

"My folks may not have much money or much schooling, but they've got their pride," replied the young mother. "WHEN THEY FOUND OUT ABOUT MY CONDITION WE TALKED IT OVER, AND EVERYONE ALLOWED AS HOW IT WAS BETTER TO HAVE A BASTARD IN THE FAMILY THAN A LAWYER."

(Well, contrary to that girl we are proud to have in our corporate family an attorney . . .)

Talk—*Action*

It is one thing to express a judgment and another to carry it out. I recall a situation when the Bishop of Winchester and Judge Mansfield were both asked to deliver speeches at their college, Balliol, in Oxford, at the 'gaudy,' a kind of Oxford alumni reunion. Afterwards, they met up at the buffet and engaged in a little banter over which of them had more influence over the common man. "Let's face it, old boy," said the bishop rather condescendingly, "in your courtroom, the worst thing you can say is 'You be hanged!' While I ultimately have far more power: to the same fellow I can declare, 'You be damned!'"

"True," conceded Judge Mansfield with a smile, "but there's a crucial difference. When I say to a man, 'YOU BE HANGED!'—HE IS!"

(Well, there is a difference between talking and doing.)

Impartial—*Merits*

I address this problem trying to be impartial. I cannot prove my impartiality the way an Oklahoma judge did. With a firm but idiosyncratic grasp of the principles of administering justice, the judge made the following pretrial statement:

"Ladies and gentlemen, in the interests of keeping all matters pertaining to this trial aboveboard, I would like to report that in my possession are two envelopes, one from the defendant containing fifteen thousand dollars and one from the plaintiff containing ten thousand—which some might call bribes. I AM THEREFORE RETURNING FIVE THOUSAND DOLLARS TO THE DEFENDANT, WHICH WILL ENABLE ME TO DECIDE THIS CASE PURELY UPON ITS MERITS."

(Let me now discuss the merits of the case . . .)

Expense—*Legal Fees*

A lawyer, Jason Sharpe, died and went to heaven. He had no sooner gotten inside the Pearly Gates then a tremendous chorus of angels began to sing gorgeously in his honor. The air was filled was a golden aura, delicious perfumes wafted everywhere, and approaching him was the tall and magnificent form of the Recording Angel smiling graciously.

"Counselor," said the Recording Angel in mellow and musical tones, "we have long been awaiting you. You are the first human being ever to break Methuselah's mark for longevity. You have lived one thousand and twenty-eight years."

"What are you talking about?" said the lawyer, astonished. "I died at the age of fifty-six."

"At the age of fifty-six?" said the Recording Angel, astonished in his turn. "Aren't you Jason Sharpe?"

"Yes."

"A lawyer?"

"Yes."

"But the Record Book has you down for one thousand and twenty-eight years."

"Sorry. Only fifty-six."

"Something must be wrong," said the Recording Angel. "Let me study the book."

He did so and suddenly clapped his hand to his forehead. "AH, I SEE WHERE WE MADE OUR MISTAKE. WE ADDED UP THE HOURS YOU CHARGED YOUR CLIENTS."

Lawyers—Determination

Years ago in Pennsylvania, I recall two farmers who were quarreling about the location of the boundary between their adjoining farms. One said, "If you don't concede that my boundary is located where I say, I will bring a suit against you in court." The other replied, "That's all right. I'll be there when the case is tried." The first said, "If I lose the case, I'll appeal to the Supreme Court of Pennsylvania." The other said, "All right, I'll be there when that appeal is heard." Then the first one said, "If I lose that case in the Supreme Court of Pennsylvania, I'll appeal to the Supreme Court of the United States." The second one said, "That's all right; I'll be there when that appeal is heard." And then the first one said, "Well, then, if I lose that case in the Supreme Court of the United States, I'll take it straight to hell." The second one said, "I WON'T BE THERE, BUT MY LAWYER WILL."

(I won't go that far but I will say that our counsel is always right there when you need him . . .)

Customs—*Outsider*

One of the worst mistakes an outsider can make is to be insensitive to the tastes and customs of the community. I recall one Philadelphia lawyer who came to Williamsport where I was practicing law in the 1960s. The Philadelphian, who was coming for business, wanted to take a deposition of my client on a certain Friday one spring.

I demurred, saying, "It would be quite impossible that particular Friday."

"What do you mean 'impossible' that Friday?" said the Philadelphia lawyer. "I'll have the judge up there subpoena him."

"Well, if you want to do that, go ahead, but I want to warn you, people in these parts don't take too kindly to that kind of high-handedness. They can't help but remember that THE LAST TIME A PERSON WAS ORDERED TO BE INTERROGATED ON A GOOD FRIDAY, THEY CRUCIFIED HIM."

Lawyer—*Ethics*

Perhaps some of you have not heard of that Aesopian fable about the blind rabbit and the blind serpent.

The serpent heard the pawsteps of the rabbit and asked, "Who's there?"

"Why don't you guess?" replied the rabbit.

"All right," answered the serpent, "but then you will have to figure out who I am."

The blind serpent said, feeling his way, "You have long ears, a quivering mouth, and a fluffy bunny tail—you must be a rabbit."

"Yes," said the blind rabbit, who now had to make his estimate. "YOU HAVE FANGS, A COLD SLIPPERY BODY THAT IS NOT STRAIGHT BUT TWISTED—YOU MUST BE A LAWYER."

BOUDOIR AND BEDCHAMBER

You must not force sex to do the work of love or love to do the work of sex.

Mary McCarthy

The bed is the poor man's opera.

Italian proverb

Love is the triumph of imagination over intelligence.

H.L. Mencken

Adultery is democracy applied to love.

H.L. Mencken

To err is human, but it feels divine.

Mae West

The difference between rape and ecstasy is salesmanship.

Lord Thompson

Woman expects that marriage will change the man but man expects that the woman will never change.

From the Humes File

Communication—*Understanding*

Not long ago I heard from an attorney about a difficulty one of his colleagues had with a client. A woman had come into the office to discuss a divorce action. The lawyer gravely addressed her. "Divorce is one of the most painful actions one can take. Of course, there are times there is no other recourse. So I must ask you what are the grounds?"

"Well," she replied, "I guess we have ten acres with a swimming pool."

"No, I don't think you quite understand me," replied the attorney. "Let me put it this way. What is the grudge you have?"

"Well," she answered, "we have a three-car garage—one for his Mercedes, my Peugeot and then the Jeep."

"I'm not sure I'm getting through to you," continued the attorney. "Let me be blunt. Did he ever beat you up?"

"Oh no," she answered. "I always rise at six o'clock every morning to prepare his breakfast."

Exasperated, the lawyer pressed on, "Why do you want a divorce?"

"YOU SEE," she replied, "WE HAVE THIS PROBLEM COMMU-NICATING."

Help—*Assistance*

All of you people here look like generous people and I know you are going to follow the advice a model gave to a friend of mine. This friend—who has recently become single again—was going to be in Los Angeles for an extended trip and so he asked a mutual friend of ours for a few good phone numbers. The evening after he landed, he called a gorgeous red-headed model named Bambi who lived in Bel Air. She said she would be delighted to meet him and gave him explicit directions on how to reach her apartment.

"When you get to Bel Air Plaza, take the lobby elevator to the seventh floor. Turn left and look for 718. When you reach my apartment, use your right elbow to ring the buzzer. When I hear that, I can release the security catch. All you have to do is put your left shoulder to the door and kick the bottom with your right foot."

"Look," said my friend, "What do you mean with all the directions, calling for an elbow, shoulder and foot?"

"BUT SURELY, DARLING," said Bambi, "YOU AREN'T GOING TO COME IN EMPTY-HANDED?"

Cost—*Misinterpretation*

Sometimes what we think is going to be bad news turns out to be the reverse. A guy told a friend of mine how his wife cornered him after dinner one night. "I don't like to pry," she said, "but something has been bothering me for days. You got a pink letter the other day. It was in a woman's handwriting. I saw you open it. You broke into a sweat. You turned white. Your hands trembled. Who was it from and what did it say?"

"Oh that," said the husband. "I decided it was best for both of us not to talk about it at the time. I've been trying to think of the best way to discuss it without causing an explosion."

"For heaven's sake, what is it?" the wife screamed.

"OKAY," replied the husband, "IT WAS FROM YOUR DRESS SHOP AND YOU OWE THEM $1,340."

(Well, I think it is high time that we discuss the sudden high costs . . .)

Help—*Assistance*

I'm going to ask for your help tonight. Now there is a right way and a wrong way to help. For an example of the wrong way, consider the second wife of an older businessman I heard about. He was a widower, she a young nightclub singer many years his junior. Shortly after the honeymoon, the husband suffered a serious heart attack.

When the young bride visited her sick mate in the hospital, she found him in an oxygen tent in the intensive care unit. The husband said to her, "Don't worry, dear. I have amply provided for you. The house, in both our names, will revert to you in the event of my death. And you know that all the stocks and bonds will go to you, meaning a principal of over two million."

"Oh, darling," cried the girl, "I am so worried about you. Is there anything I can do to help?"

"YES," he replied, "WOULD YOU MIND TAKING YOUR HAND OFF THE OXYGEN TUBE?"

(Yes, there is a right way for you to help . . .)

Recommendations—*Proposals*

A bride-to-be went to her doctor. She was marrying an 85-year-old business executive and was worried about his ardor and stamina. She went to the doctor to find out about aphrodisiacs.

"Well," replied the doctor, "the only thing I know that might be of help is oysters. Make sure he has some oysters on his wedding night."

The day after the wedding the woman returned to the doctor.

"How did it go?"

"WELL," she answered, "ONLY EIGHT OF THE DOZEN OYSTERS WORKED!"

(Well, if only a few of the recommendations work, we will be ahead of the game.)

Plans—*Failure*

Some plans don't always work out. I recall someone telling me recently about a car deal. This man had seen an advertisement in the newspaper offering a current-model Cadillac in prime condition for $50 cash. Certain it was a typographical error, the man called the advertiser out of curiosity.

To his astonishment, he found that the advertisement was legitimate. The Cadillac was indeed brand new and it was indeed in spit-and-polish condition. The title of ownership was clear and the price asked was indeed $50. The woman who was selling the car calmly accepted the five ten-dollar bills he handed her, wrote him out a receipt, and handed him the keys.

With the deal successfully concluded, the man was driven by curiosity to ask, "But why is it, madam, you have done this? This is a car worth many thousands of dollars. How can you accept fifty?"

"It's quite simple," said the woman, placing the bill of sale and the money in her purse. "MY HUSBAND DIED SHORTLY AFTER BUYING THIS CAR, AND IN HIS WILL HE DIRECTED THAT I SELL IT AND THAT THE PROCEEDS GO TO HIS MISTRESS."

(Well, the best-laid plans don't always work out the way we intended.)

Repeat—*Meeting*

A business executive, in the course of a trip to Chicago, had met a most accommodating young lady and had spent a satisfactory night with her at his hotel at which he had registered.

Or at least it *was* most satisfactory until about 3 A.M., when the young lady began to weep in heartbroken fashion.

The executive, most uneasy lest the noise of the weeping attract unwanted attention, and utterly uncertain as to what might follow, said nervously, "What's wrong, miss?"

The young lady said between sobs, "I teach school back home. I have a third-grade class, and I was just thinking what my dear little pupils would say if they knew I had made love twice in a motel room with an utter stranger."

The executive, deeply embarrassed, said, "I'm sorry, miss, to have made you feel so bad, but frankly, if we want to be absolutely accurate about this, we only made love once."

The young lady's sobs stopped instantly. She said sharply, "YOU MEAN YOU'RE NOT PLANNING TO DO IT AGAIN?"

(Well, next year we are planning another conference.)

Offense—*Defense*

Sometimes the best defense is good offense. I remember hearing at the office about a group of guys who every Wednesday played poker. One guy, having spent too many hours at the poker table the night before, showed up at the office in a haggard state. His fellow poker player nevertheless appeared spruce and sharp. He asked with concern, "What's the matter?"

The first guy said. "Listen! Coming home so late last night was bad enough, but my wife woke up and spent the rest of the night yelping at me."

"Oh, you jerk. Why did you wake her?"

"What do you mean, wake her?" he screamed. "I parked the car three blocks from the house and walked home. I took off my shoes at the corner and walked up the drive in my stocking feet. I opened the front door with an oiled key, undressed in the front hall, went up the stairs on all fours, spent ten minutes easing into the bedroom. Then I breathed, and she heard me."

"Nuts," said the other contemptuously. "Why don't you use my method? I come into the drive with my brakes squealing. I throw open the front door, shut it with a bang, turn on all the lights and go stomping up the stairs singing an old sea chantey. I whistle coming into the bedroom, slap my wife on the rump and say, 'LET'S MAKE LOVE, BABY!' AND FOR SPITE, SHE PRETENDS TO BE ASLEEP."

(Now, it's time for us to take the offensive . . .)

Severance—*Relationship*

When I was asked whether I had any second thoughts about severing our connections with this operation, I recalled the story of a husband who sat at his dying wife's bedside. "Darling," his wife breathed in little more than a whisper, "I've got a confession to make before I go. I . . . I'm the one who took the twenty thousand dollars from your safe. I spent it on a fling with your best friend, Bill. And I'm the one who reported your income-tax evasion to the government."

"THAT'S ALL RIGHT, DEAREST. DON'T GIVE IT A SECOND THOUGHT," the husband answered. "I'M THE ONE WHO POISONED YOU."

(And similarly I had no regrets about . . .)

Plans—*Results*

At a college reunion recently, I heard an alumnus catching up on the news with a fellow classmate he hadn't seen in fifteen years.

The one old grad said, "I remember our talking about the ideal woman and you said what you wanted was someone who was a princess in the living room, an economist in the kitchen and a harlot in bed. Is that what you married?"

"WELL, SORT OF," the other grad answered, "EXCEPT THAT IT TURNED OUT THAT SHE WAS A HARLOT IN THE LIVING ROOM, A PRINCESS IN THE KITCHEN AND AN ECONOMIST IN BED."

(Well, some plans don't work out the way we expected them to . . .)

Negotiations—*Demands*

In the upcoming negotiations there are some demands that are non-negotiable. I remember the time a husband said to his wife in the living room, "If I died, I would hope that you would remarry."

"Oh," his wife said, "I wouldn't think of it. We are married for eternity."

"No," he pressed. "I would not want you to be lonely."

"Oh I wouldn't want to, but if those are your wishes . . . "

For some moments there was silence. Then the husband

asked: "Dear, what would you do with my boat—my power launch?"

"I couldn't give that to anyone, it's part of you, it represents your dream."

"You'd have to give it away."

She nodded and then he inquired, "What would you do with my Ferrari sports car?"

"Honey that's an extension of yourself. I wouldn't think of it, . . . but if you insist, I suppose . . . "

"One thing more, dear . . . my golf clubs—you'd have to give those away."

She replied, "I could never do that."

"Why?" he asked.

"BECAUSE HE'S LEFT-HANDED!"

(Well, we will make some concessions but there are some demands that are non-negotiable.)

Capitalization—*Financing*

If it's a worthwhile venture it would pay us to give proper financing. I remember hearing about a mailman who was quitting his route after twenty years. He sent a letter with the news to the houses on his route. The next week as he stopped at one house to deliver the mail, he was asked by the young housewife to come in. "I have a gift for you," she said.

The mailman thanked her and she motioned him to follow. She went to the bedroom. When he hesitated, she insisted, saying, "Part of the gift is in here."

She started to disrobe and indicated to him to do likewise. He couldn't believe his good fortune. Afterwards she asked him, "Would you like some breakfast?" She soon had before him pancakes, country sausage, scrambled eggs, biscuits, jam and fresh orange juice.

He nodded. When he sat down he noted something green poking out from under the plate. He pulled it out—it was a dollar bill. "What's this for?" he asked.

"Well, when we received the letter, my husband said, 'AH, SCREW HIM . . . GIVE HIM A DOLLAR.' THE BREAKFAST WAS MY OWN IDEA!"

(So you see, if we do too little to finance this operation, we could see some unfortunate results).

Retail—*Pricing*

When I talk of pricing, I think of a computer salesman in the recent recession who saw his earnings dwindle. He had to sell the house he and his wife lived in for twenty years and they rented an apartment. Now he found it difficult to meet the monthly rent.

Before he headed out on a sales trip, he said to his wife, "I don't know what we'll do if I don't sell some equipment."

His loyal wife only a few years younger said, "I suppose I could go out on the street and sell myself."

"I hate to have you do that, but I don't know how . . . "

Three days later he returned. As he opened the door, she laid out $145.25.

"Dear, that helps, but I don't understand about the quarter."

"BUT THAT'S WHAT THEY ALL GAVE!"

(Well, we must not make the pricing of ourselves too low for the mass market . . .)

Meeting—*Morning*

It is getting late and we don't have the same advantage of a certain man who was informed by his doctor that he had only twelve more hours to live. He rushed home and told his wife, who collapsed in racking sobs. But then she pulled herself together, clasped his hands in hers, and promised, "Then

I'm going to make tonight the best night of your life, darling." She went out and bought all his favorite delicacies, opened a bottle of fine champagne, served him dinner, dressed in his favorite sexy peignoir, and led him up to bed, where she made passionate love to him.

Just as they were about to fall asleep, the husband tapped her on the shoulder. "Honey, could we make love again?"

"Sure, sweetheart," she said sleepily, and obliged.

"Once more, baby?" he asked afterwards. "It's our last night together."

"Mmmhmm," she mumbled, and they made love a third time.

"One last time, darling," he begged a little later, shaking her by the shoulder.

"Fine!" she snapped. "After all, what do you care? YOU DON'T HAVE TO GET UP IN THE MORNING!"

(Unfortunately all of us do have an early meeting tomorrow . . .)

Objection—*Refusal*

Our reaction reminds me of a young, hopeful woman I once heard at a bar coming on to an attractive young man. After he started his third daiquiri she asked, "Tell me, do you object to making love?"

"That's something I've never done," he said.

"Never made love?"

"NO, SILLY. NEVER OBJECTED."

(Well, we have no objection to the proposal . . .)

Straight Talk—*Clarity*

The other evening, I saw a rather shy guy sitting alone at the hotel bar when a beautiful young lady came and sat on the next stool. He tried to get up the nerve to strike up a conversation, but was too embarrassed to talk. So, instead, when he ordered his next drink, he ordered a second of what she was drinking and paid for them both. She nodded her thanks, but still they did not speak.

This went on for four rounds. Finally, emboldened by the liquor, he said, "Do you ever go to bed with men?"

"I NEVER HAVE BEFORE," she said, smiling, "BUT I BELIEVE YOU TALKED ME INTO IT, YOU CLEVER, SILVER-TONGUED DEVIL, YOU."

(Well, sometimes straight talk is needed.)

Location—*Site*

Sometimes it is a matter of the right location. I remember overhearing a young man approaching a beautiful young woman in a bar, and said, "You know, I hate to see a young woman like you ruin her reputation and destroy her character by hanging around a bar."

"LET ME TAKE YOU SOMEPLACE WHERE THE ATMOSPHERE IS QUIET AND MORE REFINED, LIKE MY APARTMENT."

Foreign Takeover—*Merger*

The words we're hearing are smooth but I remember what a mother once told her daughter. The daughter had gone out with some guy from abroad and she said, "Mother, he is so continental!"

"LOOK OUT," warned her mother. "CONTINENTAL MANNERS MEANS TO ME—RUSHIN' HANDS AND ROMIN' FINGERS."

(Well, there is a foreign company that's trying to get its hands . . .)

Planning—*Detail*

An aging spinster was doing her spring house cleaning. In the attic under the rafters she spotted an old lamp. She took it out and polished until the brass shined bright. Then a genie appeared.

"Ms.," he said, "you have three wishes."

"Well, first I'd like to be a beautiful young woman."

A puff of smoke—a flash of light. Suddenly she was a voluptuous, blonde young woman.

She shook herself, gazed at herself in the mirror, and then she said, "I want money—lots of money."

A puff of smoke—a flash of light. Suddenly there were cases around her of $1000 bills stacked.

The genie said, "Ms., you have one more wish."

She looked at her cat rubbing himself on her legs and said, "I wish that he was an Adonis—an Apollo of manly body and handsome face."

A puff of smoke—a flash of light. And this paragon of masculine beauty appeared before her with rugged shoulders and clean-cut, chiseled looks.

And the handsome hunk said, "NOW AREN'T YOU SORRY YOU HAD ME FIXED?"

(Well, sometimes we act before we think it out—that's how mistakes are made . . .)

BUCKINGHAM AND OTHER PALACES

In a few years there will be only five kings in the world—the King of England, the King of Spades, the King of Hearts, the King of Diamonds and the King of Clubs.

King Farouk of Egypt

All kings are mostly rapscallions.

Mark Twain

Hark! The herald angels sing. Mrs. Simpson has pinched our King.

Cleveland Amory

Here lies our Sovereign Lord and King
Whose word no man relies on
He never says a foolish thing
Nor ever does a wise one.

> Earl of Rochester, about Charles I

Monarchs are not born; they are made by artificial hallucinations.

> George Bernard Shaw

A king is entitled to no more respect than a pirate flag.

> Mark Twain

Deputy—*Job Security*

Unfortunately, in job security I am not as fortunate as King Charles II of England.

Charles had no legitimate children. That meant that his heir was his unpopular brother James, who was ineffectual and stupid.

Charles had a habit of walking about London with no concern for security, which caused his brother to protest that doing so was dangerous.

"NONSENSE," said Charles. "NO ONE IS GOING TO ASSASSINATE ME IN ORDER TO MAKE YOU KING."

(Looking at the ability of my next in command, I have no such feeling of security.)

Project—*Responsibility*

While we're all involved in this project, it is my head that is on the line if anything goes wrong. I remember the story of Henry VIII of England, who once ordered one of his courtiers to carry a message to Francis I of France. The message was an angry one and so the courtier was nervous. He said, "Francis, if angered, may decide to cut off my head."

"Have no fear," said King Henry, "for if he does, I will cut off the heads of a hundred Frenchmen in my dominion."

"So you may, your Majesty," said the courtier, "but of all the heads you cut off, not one will fit on my shoulders."

(Well, now it is my head that's on the block . . .)

Planning—*Blame*

There have been some foul-ups in the arrangements, notwithstanding our fine efforts in planning. It reminds me of the experience of the Ugandan dictator, Idi Amin. In the early 1970s he called the British High Commissioner and asked that a message be relayed to the Queen. Idi Amin wanted the Queen—who is the head of the British Commonwealth—to include Uganda in her next overseas visit. In fact, the Exalted High Potentate for Life (Amin) threatened that Uganda would leave the British Commonwealth unless the Queen scheduled a visit in the next few years. When Buckingham Palace communicated their assent, Idi Amin made extensive preparations. He had a white palatial residence built and a broad boulevard laid down leading to the Palace. Finally, he ordered a special white carriage made and purchased two white horses to draw the coach.

On the day of the Royal Visit, the Queen and Idi Amin rode in the front of the carriage up the boulevard. Suddenly one of the white horses emitted foul wind in a loud report.

Amin said, "Your Majesty, I'm so sorry. One tries to make everything so perfect . . . "

"Really," said the Queen. "I thought it was the horse."

(In this case the foul-up (I intend no pun) was due to the hotel . . .)

Retirement—*Help*

As you know, I have three years before retirement. In that regard, I think of Sir Thomas More, the English lawyer, when he was condemned to execution in 1535 for the dreadful crime of disagreeing with King Henry VIII.

As Sir Thomas approached the steps leading up to the execution block, he paused. He was rather weak from the strain of long imprisonment and he said to the executioner with typical courtesy, "I PRAY YOU, SIR, HELP ME UP THE STAIRS. AS FOR COMING DOWN, I CAN SHIFT FOR MYSELF."

(Similarly, if you can help me in these next three years, I can manage the rest of the way by myself.)

Honoree—*Responsibility*

Today we honor someone who proudly shouldered the weight of leadership. He never dodged a duty nor relinquished a responsibility. When I think of that, I recall a story about the Duke and Duchess of Windsor.

The Duke and Duchess used to spend many evenings playing bridge in their Riviera chalet when vacationing in the south of France. A guest one evening was British author Somerset Maugham, who was paired with the Duchess. During one game, she laid down her hand as dummy, Maugham upbraided her, "Dear, you didn't raise my suit when you had a king in it."

"WILLY," she replied to the author while looking at her husband, "IT IS MY EXPERIENCE THAT KINGS DO NO ONE ANY GOOD. THEY ALWAYS ABDICATE."

(Well, today we honor someone who has never abdicated his responsibility no matter how onerous . . .)

Minority—*Candor*

Politically I may be unpopular with this audience. Yet I remember what Nell Gwyn, the saucy mistress of Charles II, said. She had a rival in Louise de Kerouile, the elegant French courtesan. Once when a crowd mobbed her carriage on its way to Buckingham Palace, she emerged from its doors and cried out, "I'M NOT THE CATHOLIC WHORE, I'M NELL GWYN, THE GOOD PROTESTANT WHORE."

(Well, I'm a Democrat but a good conservative Democrat . . .)

Mistake—*Negotiation*

Winston Churchill said that we owe the Magna Charta to the vices of King John, not the least of which was lust. John had the habit of commandeering other men's wives for his own pleasure. One of those he fancied was Lord de Vescey's pretty young wife. He had de Vescey's ring copied and with that seal sent a note—purporting to be from de Vescey himself—asking the wife to come late one night to a bedroom in a town house in London where John was staying.

When word reached de Vescey he smelled a rat and hired a prostitute to take his wife's place.

A week later, at a state banquet, King John called out to the Baron at the far end of the table, "I had the pleasure of your delectable wife the other evening."

De Vescey, who later led the fight for the Magna Charta, replied. "IT WASN'T MY WIFE YOU HAD, BUT A WHORE."

(Well, if you deal in the dark, you may find that you wind up with not what you really wanted.)

Cost—*Totals*

One thing you all know is there comes a time the piper must be paid.

Edward VII, Victoria's eldest son, found this out. The one-time Prince of Wales had many paramours. One of them was Lily Langtry—known as "the Jersey Lily" (she hailed from the Island of Jersey).

One day when Mrs. Langtry was pestering Edward to buy a brooch she had seen, Edward playfully admonished her, "Lily, the amount of the jewels I have spent on you would buy a battleship."

Lily answered, "AND EDDIE, THE AMOUNT OF SE(A)MEN YOU'VE SPENT ON ME WOULD FILL IT."

[Note: This should be used with selected audiences.]

Break—Pause

When the young Prince of Wales made his first ceremonial appearance at age ten, he was taken aside by his grandfather, King Edward VII, and given this advice:

"BEING A ROYAL MEANS REMEMBERING TWO RULES: NEVER OVERLOOK ANY OPPORTUNITY TO SIT DOWN AND NEVER OVERLOOK ANY OPPORTUNITY TO RELIEVE YOURSELF."

(I think we'd all enjoy a break now . . .)

CAUCUS CHAMBER

Politics is perhaps the only profession for which no preparation is thought necessary.

Robert Louis Stevenson

A man who is not a liberal at sixteen has no heart. A man who is not a conservative at sixty has no head.

Benjamin Disraeli

The cheaper the politician the more he costs the country.

W.R. Inge

I never looked on public office as a form of social security.

Sen. Edmund Muskie

An honest politician is one who when bought stays bought.

Simon Cameron

Politics ain't beanbag.

Finley Peter Dunne

Senatorial courtesy means the Senators stop calling each other names after the elections.

Art Linkletter

A statesman is any politician it is safe to name a school after.

From the Humes File

A statesman lives to serve his country well—a politician serves to live well.

From the Humes File

Mess—*Choice*

There is no law saying we have to continue the course we have been taking. Take it from the words of Calvin Coolidge.

Just after the First World War, a debate occurred in the Massachusetts state legislature in which passions were hotly aroused. In fact, one senator used the unparliamentary expression "Go to Hell." The object of the profanity called on the then Lieutenant Governor, Calvin Coolidge, to see if there were some rules calling for a reprimand. Coolidge, as the presiding officer of the Senate, replied, "SENATOR, I'VE LOOKED UP THE LAW AND YOU DON'T HAVE TO GO THERE."

(And we don't have to continue to go blindly down the path to perdition that we have been following either.)

Similarity—*Difference*

Speaker of the House Nicholas Longworth was totally bald, but this did not inhibit his way with the ladies.

When a Congressional colleague ran his hand over Longworth's bald head and said, "It feels just like my wife's behind," Longworth passed his own hand over his head and said, "MY HEAVENS, SO IT DOES."

(Well, today, though the situation feels the same as the one we faced last year . . .)

Hospitality—*Warmth*

At the reception earlier tonight I again had the experience of enjoying your warm welcome and outgoing hospitality. In fact, I might characterize you by the phrase once used to describe a former senator.

Back in the 1950 senatorial primary campaign in Florida, veteran Claude Pepper was opposed by George Smathers, Pepper was especially strong in the "Bible belt," or northern, section of Florida. To shake the hold Pepper had on these people, Smathers developed a special speech making use of the facts that Pepper was a bachelor, a Harvard Law School graduate, had a niece who was a staff member of a Senate subcommittee, and a sister who acted in New York.

For the county courthouse rallies, Smathers would say, "Are you aware, my friends, that in his youth Claude Pepper was found matriculating in Harvard and that he has habitually indulged in *celibacy*. Not only that, he has practiced *nepotism* in Washington, with his own niece; and he has a sister who is a *thespian* in wicked Greenwich Village in New York. Worst of all, my friends, CLAUDE PEPPER IS KNOWN ALL OVER WASHINGTON FOR HIS LATENT TENDENCY TOWARD OVERT EXTROVERSION."

(Ladies and gentlemen, after attending the reception

tonight, I think I can say there is nothing latent about your overt extroversion.)

Politics—*Promises*

Will Rogers once told about a Congressman who prepared a speech but then didn't have a chance to deliver it. He asked and received permission to have the speech printed in the Congressional Record. The speech promised highways and economic prosperity. At the places where he expected applause, the congressman wrote in the word *applause*. The printer, unfortunately, had trouble reading the congressman's handwriting. EVERY PLACE WHERE IT SHOULD HAVE READ *applause*, THE PRINTER HAD INSERTED THE WORD *applesauce* INSTEAD.

Personnel—*Jobs*

Many years ago, when Arizona first came into the Union, Senator Harry Ashurst said during his maiden speech in the Senate, "Mr. President, the baby state I represent has the greatest potential. This state could become a paradise. We need only two things—water and lots of good people."

Boies Penrose, a senior senator from Pennsylvania, begged to interrupt: "IF THE SENATOR WILL PARDON ME FOR SAYING SO, THAT'S ALL THEY NEED IN HELL."

(Well, companies like mine don't need water but we can always use some good men and women . . .)

Brevity—*Speech*

I plan to be brief because I know there is nothing more agonizing than a long speech at a time like this. It brings to mind what a condemned man said back at the turn of the century in Dodge City. Just as the hanging was about to take place, a candidate for Congress shoved his way through the crowd to a place near the gallows.

As the sheriff was adjusting the rope, he said to the hanging victim, "You have ten minutes to live. Perhaps you would like to say something to the crowd."

The prisoner shook his head, sullenly indicating that he would not like to say anything. Whereupon the congressional aspirant jumped up on the gallows, opened his coat, and cried, "If the gentleman does not want his ten minutes, will he kindly yield to me, I should like to begin by saying, if elected to Congress, I . . . "

That was too much for the prisoner. "SHERIFF," he said, "I CAME HERE TO BE HANGED, NOT TORTURED. PULL THE ROPE!" And they did.

(Well, I don't propose to torture anyone with a long speech; I only want to stress a few points.)

Bureaucrat—*Public Office*

When you mention that I am a public official with high responsibility, I think of the other day when I was in the capital doing an errand for an aggrieved citizen. I drove down and looked for a parking place. The spots reserved for officials were all used, so I parked in a "no parking" zone. Under the windshield wiper, I left a note: "I drove around the block five times—no space. I have a public duty to perform for my constituents or else I'll lose my job. (Signed) Forgive us our trespasses."

When I returned, there was a parking ticket—and also a note: "I'VE BEEN ON THIS BEAT FIVE YEARS. I HAVE A DUTY TO DO FOR THE PEOPLE OR ELSE I'LL LOSE MY JOB. (SIGNED) LEAD US NOT INTO TEMPTATION."

(I hope that what I say today is going to lead no one astray.)

Support—*Hypocrisy*

The concern shown by some of my opponents reminds me of the remark of Woodrow Wilson at the time of his valiant fight for the League of Nations, which ruined his health to a point where rumors hinted that his mind had been affected.

Senator Albert Fall, a bitter Republican foe of Wilson, called at the White House to see what truth there might be in these rumors. "Well, Mr. President," was Fall's greeting, "we all have been praying for you."

Wilson answered, "WHICH WAY, SENATOR?"

(And I might question the concern . . .)

Anniversary—*Husband*

The members of the Women's National Democratic Club surprised the wife of Senator Fritz Hollings with a presentation on her wedding anniversary.

His wife, Betty, rose and said she owed the success of her marriage to the fact that both she and her husband shared the same passions.

"YOU SEE," she added, "WE'RE BOTH IN LOVE WITH THE SAME GUY."

Misstatement—*Promises*

On the issue of the League of Nations, Senator William Borah railed against President Woodrow Wilson. When Wilson was asked about the Senator's populist attacks, he replied, "THE SENATOR HAS SUCH AN ESTEEM FOR TRUTH, HE SPENDS HIS WHOLE LIFE EMBELLISHING IT."

Politics—*Expensive*

The son of Lord Chesterfield wrote his father about seeking a career in Parliament.

Chesterfield wrote back, "THE PURSUIT OF OFFICE IS LIKE

THE PURSUIT OF WOMAN—THE POSITION RIDICULOUS, THE EXPENSE DAMNABLE AND THE PLEASURE FLEETING."

Reactionary—*Mean-Spirited*

Some years ago in Congress some Republicans were attacking the rising rate of illegitimacy and its cost to the welfare program.

Democratic Congressman Eckhart of Texas rose and said, "I THINK THERE'S TOO MUCH FOCUS ON THE NATURAL BASTARDS AND NOT ENOUGH ON THE SELF-MADE ONES."

Name—*Mistake*

A sexagenarian senator for the South married a young woman who marvelled at her husband's ability to remember names. He said, "Honey, I do it by associating the name with the person's most prominent feature: a pug nose, blonde hair or maybe what he does or where he's from.

"For example, you know, Ed Lilley? Well, when I found out his mother was from Philadelphia, I said 'Lilley from Philly.'" Now, Tom Hook actually has a pug nose, but I still said to myself, 'Hook who doesn't have a hook nose.' Or there's Tony Fungio, who's an undertaker. I said to myself, 'Fungi who has fun at funerals.' It's easy, once you get the knack of it."

At a bar association convention, his young wife met for a moment Mrs. Hamilton Womack, the head of the State Bar Association Auxiliary. She was a woman of imposing girth. The Senator's wife thought and said to herself, "Mrs. Womack with the big fat stomach."

The next night at the top of the stairs before descending into the ballroom, she recognized the Bar Auxiliary dowager and said to her husband . . .

"DEAR, I'D LIKE TO INTRODUCE YOU TO MRS. KELLY."

(Well, I have a similar kind of problem for my name is mistakenly associated with . . .)

Stupidity—*Jackass*

When Champ Clark was Speaker of the House, Congressman Johnson of Indiana interrupted the speech of an Ohio representative, calling him a jackass. The expression was ruled to be unparliamentary and Johnson apologized.

"I withdraw the unfortunate word, Mr. Speaker, but I insist that the gentleman from Ohio is out of order."

"How am I out of order?" angrily shouted the other.

Congressman Johnson replied, "PROBABLY A VETERINARIAN COULD TELL YOU." And that was allowed to enter the Congressional Record.

(Perhaps a veterinarian could explain how we got into the mess we face today.)

COUNTRY LANES

Italians come to ruin generally in three ways—women, gambling and farming. My family chose the slowest one.

Pope John XXIII

What you farmers ought to do is raise less corn and more hell.

I have no love for the country, it is a healthy grave.

Sydney Smith

You can take the boy out of the country, but you can't take the country out of the boy.

Arthur (Bugs) Baer

A good farmer is nothing more than a handyman with a good sense of humor.

E.B. White

The problem of poverty on the farms of America is low income.

Nelson Rockefeller

If you work long and hard enough on a farm, you can make a fortune—that is if you strike oil.

From the Humes File

Costs—*Outside Services*

Our rising costs are due to purchased services, some of which should be done at the in-house level. This situation reminds me of the man who came from poor mountain folk in eastern Kentucky and climbed to the head of one of the Fortune 500 companies.

The CEO, while in Tokyo, got a call from his office. They had received a wire from Kentucky stating that his father had died.

Because his family had no phone, he wired to the nearby general store, "Spare no expense in funeral arrangement. Cannot come home. In midst of a merger negotiation in Tokyo."

Some while after he arrived home, he got a bill from the family for $6,500.

He promptly paid it. But the next month he got another bill for $100. Thinking that it was some incidental expense left over, he sent a check to cover it.

The next month another bill came asking for $100. Again he paid it.

When another bill for $100 came the next month, he called the general store and told them he would talk to his brother the next day. When that day came, he asked his brother, "What's this continuing bill for $100?"

Replied the brother, "WELL, WE GOT PAPPY IN THAT SATIN-LINED MAHOGANY COFFIN AND HE DIDN'T LOOK RIGHT IN HIS MOUNTAIN SHIRT AND PANTS. SO WE RENTED A TUXEDO!

Region—*Hallmark*

When the chairman mentioned the various things this community is known for, I couldn't help but remember a story Lyndon Johnson told about himself. In the time of his deepest unpopularity, LBJ told of an easterner, a Republican, who was doing some business near Johnson City, Texas. One day after he finished work for the day he drove out of his motel in ranch country to the nearest bar. He ordered a double martini on the rocks. When he finished it, he had enough liquid courage to express what he had always wanted to. So in loud tones he stood up and yelled, "Lyndon Johnson is a horse's ass!"

He had no sooner sat down when a big mean hombre at the end of the bar marched down, picked him up and threw him out of the swinging doors. The next day when he was through with his business he got to wondering about the way he had been treated. He knew this was the area Johnson was from, but after all, it is a free country. So, teeth clenched, he went back into the same saloon. This time he ordered two double martinis, one right after the other. Thus fortified, he slowly got to his feet, looked down the length of the bar and yelled again, "Lyndon Johnson is a horse's ass!"

Right away another big hombre stalked down the floor. "Wait a minute," said the easterner. "Why can't I say the President is a horse's ass? After all, this is a free country, isn't it?"

"You don't understand, mister," said the hombre. "This is horse country."

Trends—*Conclusion*

We have seen enough data from market trends to sense what will be happening. I remember the case when a man was charged with shooting a number of prize quail being raised on a farmer's adjoining piece of woodland. The counsel for the defense opted for an aggressive opening. "Tell me, sir," she challenged, "are you prepared to swear that that man shot your quail?"

"Hold your horses, young woman," rejoined the farmer calmly. "I said I suspected him of shooting my birds."

"Ah hah!" crowed the attorney. "And just why is it that you came to suspect that gentleman in particular?"

"First of all, I heard a gun go off and saw some quail fall out of the sky," retorted the farmer testily. "Second, well, onto my property I came across that very fellow with a gun and a bird dog. Third, I found three of my quail in his pocket . . . AND I DON'T RECKON THEY FLEW IN THERE AND COMMITTED SUICIDE."

Efficiency—*Expense*

I find that we have been stacking up costs by duplicating and even triplicating the same services. It reminds me of the time in the Kentucky mountains when the old farmer came home to find his wife in the arms of her lover. Mad with rage, he shot her dead. The Kentucky jury brought in a verdict of justifiable homicide.

Just as he was about to leave the courtroom a free man, the judge stopped him and asked, "Why did you shoot your wife instead of her lover?"

"JUDGE," he replied, "I DECIDED IT WAS BETTER TO SHOOT A WOMAN ONCE THAN A DIFFERENT MAN EACH WEEK."

(Well, it is cheaper for us to . . .)

Financing—*Short-term*

A meter inspector from the Rural Cooperative while visiting a farm noticed a pig in the backyard limping around on a peg leg.

"What happened to the pig?"

"Well, Betsy is a splendid pig. Why, when our house caught fire one night, she oinked so loud, she woke us and we got the fire truck in time to save the house."

"I can see that she is special."

"Not only that but when my youngest fell in the pond, she squealed so loud, we were able to save her from drowning."

"Yes, but I still don't understand why Betsy has the peg leg."

"CAN'T YOU UNDERSTAND?" He asked. "WHY, SHE'S PART OF THE FAMILY! WE COULDN'T EAT HER ALL AT ONE TIME."

(Similarly, I think it's a pity if we sell off parts of this popular and successful operation for a short-term gain.)

Consumers—*Directions*

A western settler with a spread was traveling with a wagon to buy supplies when he was ambushed by a band of Indians. They took him back to their camp and prepared him for the cruelest form of death. They stripped him, coated him with honey and tied him to an anthill. When he begged for release, the chief said, "White man, if you prove yourself equal to a Chippewa brave, we will let you go."

"What do I have to do?"

"First you must drink a jug of fire water. Then you have to ride that mustang bareback until it's broken in. If you succeed in that you go to the brown tepee and wrestle a bear until you pin it to the mat. After that, you must go to the grey tent and make love to an Indian maiden.

"Give me the firewater," he said as they released him. Draining the jug, he stumbled out to ride the wild horse. When the bucking bronco slowed to a walk, he alit dizzy from the effects of the bronco ride and booze. He reeled his way to the two tepees.

Finally, bloody from gashes and claw marks, he crawled out of the second tent toward the chief.

"RASSLIN' WITH THAT PRETTY INDIAN GIRL WASN'T A PROBLEM, BUT THAT BEAR SHORE DIDN'T WANT TO MAKE LOVE."

(Well, similarly you can't make a customer buy what he doesn't like . . .)

License—Annulment

I remember the case of the young mountaineer who came in to see a lawyer in the county seat. "I want a divorce."

"Divorce?" responded the lawyer. "But you were married at the courthouse by the Justice of the Peace only last week. What's wrong?"

"There was no license," replied the irate groom.

"No marriage license? Well that's certainly grounds for . . . "

"NO, I MEAN NO GUN LICENSE. HER DADDY DIDN'T HAVE A LICENSE FOR THE SHOTGUN HE WAS CARRYING."

(Unlike that father we have the license [or should I say franchise] for this area.)

DEPARTURE LOUNGE

Worth seeing? Yes. But not worth going to see.

Samuel Johnson

In America there are two classes of travel—first class and with children.

Robert Benchley

You can't take it with you, but just try to travel without it.

From the Humes File

Travel is broadening—especially if you stop at all the recommended eating places.

From the Humes File

A tourist is a person who travels to find things that are different and then complains when they are.

From the Humes File

Too often, travel, instead of broadening the mind, merely
lengthens the conversation.

From the Humes File

Break—*Recess*

Two gentlemen, both hard of hearing and strangers to each
other, were on a train. One of them, peering at the station they
were entering, said, "Pardon me, sir, but is this Wembley?"

"No," said the other. "Actually, it's Thursday."

"SO AM I," said the first, "LET'S STOP FOR A DRINK."

[Note: This should only be attempted if you can imitate
an upper-class British accent.]

Safety—*Caution*

A friend of mine who recently was flying from San Francisco
to Los Angeles noticed that the Fasten Seat Belt sign was
kept lit during the whole journey, although the flight was a
particularly smooth one.

The stewardess explained, "We have 25 of the Mets baseball team on board because their charter plane had engine
trouble. Then we have 15 finalists for the Miss America
pageant going to Los Angeles for the choosing of Miss California . . . WHAT WOULD YOU DO?"

(Similarly I think caution is in order . . .)

Capitalization—*Direction*

I'm all for growth but not for financing expansion for expansion's sake, without really knowing where it will lead us. I
like to explore new opportunities but I am no Christopher
Columbus:

"YOU KNOW—HE SET OFF NOT KNOWING WHERE HE WAS GOING AND WHEN HE GOT THERE HE DIDN'T KNOW WHERE HE WAS AND HE DID IT ALL ON BORROWED MONEY."

Option—*Overseas*

We have some options before us. Fortunately we are not like the Soviet travel agent at the convention of travel agents in Moscow in the 1960s.

An English representative and French agent invited this Russian Intourist official for dinner. After some vodka, the discussion turned to their own personal travel preferences.

The Englishman said, "I'd like to fly and spend my extra time sightseeing in cities." The Frenchman countered, "For me, I'd like to rent a sports car and drive it with the top down across the land."

"For me," said Ivan, "I'll take a tank."

"A tank?" replied the other two.

"WELL, THE TANK IS THE ONLY WAY WE RUSSIANS TRAVEL ABROAD."

(Well, unlike the Russians, we have many choices if we want to expand overseas.)

Friends—*Supporter*

We all have our own ideas of man's best friend. I know the choice of a friend of mine who recently took a vacation mountain climbing in the Alps with a native Swiss guide. On the windy, snowy slopes, my friend and his guide temporarily lost their bearings for a bit and in the bitter cold were preparing camp when all at once they sighted the familiar Saint Bernard dog trotting along with a keg tied around its neck.

The Swiss guide said, "Here comes man's best friend."

"YES," said the American, "AND LOOK AT THE BIG FUZZY DOG THAT'S BRINGING IT."

(That may be one view of man's best friend, but I know some who will testify that this organization certainly has a great friend in . . .)

Mess—*Incapability*

There are those who think the situation today holds out little hope of improvement. Their judgment is not unlike that made by a British admiral years ago of an Anglican bishop. The two had gone to school at Eton before World War I. Both were brilliant students, bitter in their rivalry; both went on to great success. One became distinguished as an admiral in the Royal Navy; the other a ranking bishop of the Church of England. Though many years passed, their hate for each other remained undiminished. Years later they encountered each other in London's Liverpool Street station. The bishop went over to the admiral in his dark blue uniform and all his braid, and spoke haughtily.

"I say, Conductor, which is the next train to Manchester?"

The admiral, looking at the portly bishop in his belted clerical cassock, replied, "MADAM, IN YOUR CONDITION, I SHOULDN'T THINK YOU WOULD BE GOING ANYWHERE."

(With the condition we find society in today, we might wonder where we are going . . .)

Session—*Weariness*

As anyone who has lived in New York knows, subway riders in the Big Apple are not noted for the ease with which they give up their seats to those who need them. Some years ago I saw this businessman in his 50s, possibly a stockbroker, take a seat and then bury himself behind the newspaper, paying no attention to any woman or elderly person who might be standing in front of him.

After five stops, a young woman in this crowded train

leaned over his paper and said, "Pardon me, sir, but I'm pregnant. Could you let me have your seat?"

Embarrassed, the stockbroker jumped up. The woman sat down and the businessman seized the strap in his turn, holding his newspaper with the other hand. It was not very long, however, before it dawned on him that the young lady who had taken his seat had a slim figure, very slim indeed.

Outraged, he leaned over and said, "Young lady, how long have you been pregnant?"

And she said, "HALF AN HOUR. AND BOY, AM I POOPED!"

(Well, our sessions and workshops today have lasted over three hours this afternoon and we're pooped and ready for some rest.)

Uniqueness—*Change*

After Ulysses S. Grant served eight years as president, he commenced a world-wide tour. A reporter caught up with him in Venice and asked him what he thought of the city famed for its gondolas.

Grant answered, "IT WOULD BE A GREAT CITY IF IT WERE DRAINED."

(Well, we don't think we should tamper with an institution that is unique . . .)

Qualifications—*Honoree*

A computer salesman was on stand-by at the airport. Finally his name was called to take the last seat on the airplane. His luck was magnificent when he saw who his seatmate was for the two hour trip—a stunning woman whose reading glasses did not veil her beauty and whose severely tailored business suit did not succeed in concealing her voluptuous figure. He tried to engage her in polite conversation about the weather but only received a stare for his efforts.

Unfortunately, she kept her attention on the reports she

was reading. When the flight attendant offered drinks, she took a cola and he a vodka. Somewhat later, in arranging her papers, a bump in the flight caused her to spill her drink on the salesman's lap.

Greatly flustered, she profusely apologized, and then added, "I'm sorry if I seemed rude. You see I'm caught up in my work and I don't have much time for socializing. Anyway, I'm very particular about men."

The salesman asked, "Well what do you look for?"

"There are three types that attract me: American Indians for one—they are so virile and reputed to possess great stamina. I guess I'm also attracted to Jewish men. They are good listeners, sensitive to a woman's moods and very generous. And then I guess I like doctors because they know so much about a woman's body."

"By the way," she added, "my name is Sylvia Williams, what's yours?"

He thought quickly and said, "TONTO BERNSTEIN, M.D."

(Well, tonight we honor someone who doesn't have to falsify his credentials because he has all the right qualifications.)

First Prize—*Award*

Two American schoolteachers ended up their summer vacation in Britain by going to the Edinburgh Festival.

One afternoon, in the small park just above Princess Street, they saw a Scotsman resplendent in his kilt sleeping on a park bench. He reeked of the rich malt that is the prime product of that country, and he was snoring happily on the park bench, oblivious to everything.

The one teacher said to the other, "You know I always wanted to know what a Scotsman wore under his kilt."

"So did I. Do you think we can just peek under the kilt to find out?"

Ever so gently the one woman lifted the kilt. And there they saw that he was in his altogether.

Then the other woman said, "You know we ought to leave something to signify that we have discovered the Scotsman's secret."

"But what could we leave?" asked the other, putting her hand to her head while searching for an answer. Then she touched on her blue hair ribbon and said, "That's it!"

While the one teacher gently raised the kilt again, the other took her blue ribbon from her hair and tied it around the only thing around which something could be tied. Then they left, happy that they had left behind a token of their discovery.

A half an hour later, the Scotsman, feeling some constraint in his nether parts, lifted his kilt and exclaimed, "OH MY, I DON'T KNOW WHERE YOU'VE BEEN, BUT I'M PROUD YOU CAME AWAY WITH FIRST PRIZE!"

(Well, today we give a blue ribbon to . . .)

[Note: This story is only proper for selected audiences. A Scottish brogue helps.]

Technology—*Change*

In the last decade of the 19th century, the bishop of the Methodist Church in Ohio was widely known for his scholarly sermons, published writings and lectures.

One day, at a talk at an Ohio college, the Bishop propounded that everything about nature had already been discovered and that all useful inventions had already been made.

Afterwards a professor questioned him, saying that he thought the bishop was mistaken. "Why, in a few years," he said, "we'll be able to fly through the air."

"What a nonsensical idea!" the bishop said. "Flight," he

assured the professor, "is reserved for the birds and the angels."

FORTUNATELY THE ADVICE ON THAT SUBJECT BY BISHOP WRIGHT WAS NOT BELIEVED BY HIS SONS, WILBUR AND ORVILLE.

Communication—*Clarity*

In times of stress or excitement, we are not always as articulate as we would like to be. I recall the shy young man who had to fly to Pittsburgh. He entered the airline ticket office and the girl with an hourglass figure was behind the counter. She was wearing a low-cut dress and bending low over notations she was making. He stared at her.

She looked up, and said, "What can I do for you, sir?"

The young man could hear his own breath hissing in his ears like steam, but tried to master the situation. He did, after all, need two tickets to Pittsburgh. He finally stuttered.

"UH, GIVE ME TWO PICKETS TO . . . "

Statistics—*Ratio*

The statistics cited recall an exchange that took place in a fast food stop in Myrtle Beach. An old man was slowly picking through his plate of salad when a young boy from a family seated at a nearby table approached him.

"Where do you live, Mister?" asked the lad. "We come from Pennsylvania."

"Myrtle Beach," was the old man's curt answer.

"Gee that's great," continued the boy. "How long have you lived here?"

"All my life," was the dour reply.

"Gee that's great—how long is that?"

"Eighty-seven years," the old man sighed wearily.

"Gee that's really great."

"Do you mean," the old man asked, "because I managed to live eighty-seven years?"

"No," said the boy. "Because I read that at eighty-seven there are eight women for every man."

"SON," replied the octogenarian, "THAT'S THE MOST USELESS STATISTIC I EVER HEARD."

(Well, the statistics I will quote are not useless.)

Progress Report

A corporate friend of mine likes to go moose-hunting in Quebec every August. Last year he and his friend flew to Quebec City and then hired a pilot to fly them in this small Cessna to the northern woods.

The pilot said, "In a week I will be back to pick you up. But you can't shoot more than one moose. If you shoot two, the plane won't be able to fly."

In a week the plane landed on the clearing beside a lake. To his dismay the two hunters proudly displayed two moose they had shot.

"But I warned you," he said, "the plane won't get off the ground."

The pilot shook his head and they boarded the small plane with the two moose.

The plane made a wobbly take-off and then sputtered and crashed into some trees. My friend was knocked out by the collision. Hours later he came to life and he asked his hunting companion groggily, "Where am I?"

And the answer was, "ABOUT 20 YARDS FURTHER THAN LAST YEAR."

(Well, we have had a little more progress to report on . . .)

DRESSING ROOM

I deny that I ever said actors are cattle; what I said was that actors should be treated like cattle.

Alfred Hitchcock

Strip away the phony tinsel of Hollywood and you find the real tinsel underneath.

Oscar Levant

Hollywood is like Picasso's bathroom.

Candice Bergen

Hollywood is a trip through a sewer in a glass-bottomed boat.

Wilson Mizner

To be an actor and get paid for it is one way of turning conceit into profit.

From the Humes File

The critics were biased. They saw it at a disadvantage—the curtain was up.

From the Humes File

Architect—*Planner*

One of the most sensational trials in American history occurred when millionaire Harry Thaw shot architect Stanford White in a quarrel over the lovely Evelyn Nesbit, the Girl in the Velvet Swing. Thaw was given ten years in prison. Shortly after he was released, he attended the grand opening of the Roxy Theater in New York. As he gazed in horror at the Hollywood-Byzantine baroque style of the lobby, he gasped, "MY GOD, I SHOT THE WRONG ARCHITECT!"

(Fortunately we didn't choose the wrong one to make our plans . . .)

Criticism—*Response*

I have a copy of the newspaper article and I have a mind to do with it what Tallulah Bankhead once did. In answer to a highly uncomplimentary review of a performance, the actress wrote this note to the critic: "I AM SITTING IN THE SMALLEST ROOM OF THE HOUSE. YOUR REVIEW IS BEFORE ME. SOON IT WILL BE BEHIND ME."

(Well, I am not going to let some half-assed criticism . . .)

Return—*Retirement*

Johnny Carson, the quintessential talk show host of the twentieth century, is a man with a deep distrust of the press. Every now and then, however, he has been known to loosen up and give hungry reporters something to report.

That's what he did while visiting Harvard to receive an award. It was one of the rare times that Carson subjected himself to the sometimes inane questions of the press, and he maintained his cool demeanor throughout.

One desperate reporter asked, "What would you like to have inscribed on your tombstone?"

Carson quipped, "I'LL BE RIGHT BACK."

Appreciation—*Honoree*

One evening, Bette Davis was part of a dinner party that included a fabulously beautiful woman who sat at the table, rarely speaking, but presenting a perfect profile for the breathless admiration of every man in the place.

At another table was a friend of Miss Davis. Hastily, he scribbled a note and sent it to her by way of the waiter. Miss Davis opened the note, which read. "My God, Bette, who is that incredibly gorgeous creature at your table?"

Bette Davis scrawled an answer; the waiter carried it back to the questioner. He opened it hastily and found written there, "ME!!!"

(Unlike Bette Davis I have had more than enough attention tonight . . .)

Study—*Caution*

Playwright George S. Kaufman was once unfortunate enough to be sitting in front of a nonstop talker at the theater. The moment she took her seat, the woman began holding forth on the decor of the theater, the appearance of certain members of the audience, the high price of tickets, and everything else that came to mind. During the first act, she passed judgment on the dialogue, the set and the talents of the actors, all loudly enough for everyone in the vicinity to hear.

As the curtain fell and the house lights went up, the woman told her companion how much she hated standing in the lobby during intermission and how she was equally displeased at the prospect of sitting in her seat without the chance to stretch her legs.

Kaufman turned in his seat and frowned at her. "MADAM," he said, "DO YOU EVER HAVE AN UNEXPRESSED THOUGHT?"

(Well, I don't think off-the-cuff opinions will give us the answer. I suggest a study be made.)

Pomposity—*Leadership*

Few people in Hollywood doubted that Orson Welles had enormous talent, especially in the days following the release of *Citizen Kane*, which many believe to be the best American film ever made. However, no one had as high an opinion of Welles' talent as the great man himself. Summing up Welles' self-image, Herman Mankiewicz, who co-wrote the screenplay for *Citizen Kane*, one day pointed to Welles and grumbled, "THERE BUT FOR GOD, GOES GOD."

(Well, our honoree has never confused arrogance with authority or position with pomposity.)

President—*Founder*

Some of you might not know that William Shakespeare performed as an actor as well as a playwright. Yet he was not the star performer of his company. The matinee idol of that time was Richard Burbage. In Shakespeare's drama, *Richard III*, Burbage played the hunchbacked King.

In the makeshift dressing room Burbage put on the door "King Richard III."

After one performance a woman groupie infatuated with Burbage knocked on the door and said, "Is this King Richard?" Yet unbeknownst to the fan, Shakespeare had gotten to the room first and it was his voice that answered her.

"NO IT IS NOT KING RICHARD, BUT KING WILLIAM AND YOU SHOULD UNDERSTAND THAT IN ROYAL PRECEDENT WILLIAM THE CONQUEROR MUST COME BEFORE RICHARD III."

(Well, if the founder of the British Royal House was William the Conqueror, the founder of our 'house' . . .)

Self-Improvement—*Change*

Champion boxer Rocky Graziano wore his lack of education like a badge. When his boxing days were over and he was trying to make a transition into movies and commercials, someone suggested that he study at the Actor's Studio.

"Why should I go to a place like that?" Graziano asked. He then added, "ALL THEY DO IS TEACH GUYS LIKE MARLON BRANDO AND PAUL NEWMAN TO TALK LIKE ME."

(Well, we are never too old to learn.)

Quality—*Reputation*

We are known for our quality products and should not risk cheapening our image. I recall the story of Margot Asquith, the handsome wife of British Prime Minister Lord Herbert Henry Asquith, whose beauty was matched by her barbed tongue.

When she and movie star Jean Harlow met for the first time, Harlow was careless enough to address the lady by her first name. To make matters worse, Harlow mispronounced the name sounding the "t" as in Mar-got.

Lady Asquith drew herself up to her full height and corrected Harlow by saying, "MY DEAR, THE 'T' IN MY NAME, 'MARGOT,' IS SILENT, AS IN 'HARLOW.'"

(There is a difference between 'quality' and 'tawdry' and we intend to maintain . . .)

Cause—*Obesity*

It is said that the lanky vegetarian George Bernard Shaw once met Alfred Hitchcock in London. As is well known, Hitchcock was no Spartan when it came to the delights of the table and his girth was proof of his appetite.

When they met, Hitchcock said, "To look at you, Mr. Shaw, one would think there already was famine in England."

Shaw shot back, "AND TO LOOK AT YOU, ONE WOULD THINK YOU HAD CAUSED IT."

(Now well it may look as if we were responsible for the recent setback . . .)

Overcaution—*Bold*

While Eugene Field was drama critic on the old *Denver Post*, he was given an assignment to report on a performance of *King Lear*. His review was brief but pointed:

"Last night at the Tabor Opera House, *King Lear* was played. THE ACTOR PLAYED THE KING AS THOUGH UNDER THE PREMONITION THAT SOMEONE WAS ABOUT TO PLAY THE ACE."

(Well, in this venture we have to be bold and authoritative.)

Preference—*Technique*

As we all know, there is a right way to do everything, and the success of an operation depends upon its perfect execution. I remember hearing a story about John Barrymore, who was a connoisseur of martinis. Once when he was ordering his favorite drink, he told the bartender, "Very dry. Thirty parts gin to one part vermouth."

"All right, Mr. Barrymore," said the bartender. "Shall I twist a bit of lemon peel over it?"

"MY GOOD MAN, WHEN I WANT LEMONADE, I'LL ASK FOR IT."

(And similarly, if we don't want an operation watered down . . .)

Cost—*Expensive*

For that cost we should be getting a lot more. It reminds me of the time the famous Zsa Zsa Gabor went shopping at the fabulous Neiman-Marcus department store. Zsa Zsa was anxious to buy some pajamas for her uncle. She picked out a style she liked and asked the cost.

"Two hundred dollars, ma'am," said the clerk.

"TWO HUNDRED DOLLARS!" gasped Zsa Zsa. "FOR THAT MONEY THEY SHOULD COME WITH A MAN IN THEM!"

(And for the amount we're paying, we should get . . .)

Unexpected—*Summons*

In the early 1940s the temperamental John Barrymore and tempestuous Tallulah Bankhead were sometimes paired together on the stage. Even though both shared a passion for gin, they despised each other.

Once, to rattle Barrymore, Tallulah paid a stage hand to make the telephone ring on stage next to the chair in which Barrymore was sitting.

When the unscripted call came in on stage, Barrymore picked up the telephone receiver and looked at Tallulah watching him slyly across the stage and called out:

"IT'S FOR YOU, DEAR!"

(Well, we have had an unexpected challenge handed to us—but unlike Barrymore we cannot delegate it away or pass it off . . .)

Problem—*Difficulty*

P.T. Barnum had a problem. His museum of curiosities and strange animals in New York was so popular that the long lines outside discouraged some would-be customers. He had to find some way to make sure his patrons didn't linger so long inside, so he rigged up a corridor toward a doorway to the street and displayed above it prominently the sign, "TO THE EGRESS."

(Well, I'm sure we'd like to find the 'egress' or exit out of the box we find ourselves in today.)

Tension—*Worry*

I understand there is some concern about the situation. I seem to see more nail-biters at staff meetings. The British-born movie actor David Niven was a habitual nail-biter. Once he received a postcard written by his friend, Noel Coward, who was traveling in Italy. The card showed a picture of the Venus de Milo and said, "YOU SEE WHAT WILL HAPPEN IF YOU KEEP ON BITING YOUR NAILS."

Private—*Embarrassment*

I think we should keep our planning discussions private. I recall relating what happened when Jane Wyman was entertaining very special guests. After looking over all the appointments carefully, the morning before, she put a note on the guest towels, "If you use these I will murder you." It was meant for her then-husband, Ronald Reagan. In the excitement she forgot to remove the note. After the guests had departed, the towels were discovered, still in perfect order, as well as the note itself.

(Well, we would be well advised not to put down on paper . . .)

EMBASSY PARTY

An ambassador is a man of virtue sent to lie abroad for his country.

Sir Henry Wooton

The requisites of a diplomat are self-control, protocol and alcohol.

Adlai Stevenson

Diplomats are only useful in fair weather; when it rains they drown in every raindrop.

Charles de Gaulle

A diplomat is a man who tries never to stand between a dog and a lamppost.

From the Humes File

A diplomat is one who can hold his tongue in several languages.

From the Humes File

To say nothing while speaking is half of the art of diplomacy.

From the Humes File

Mistake—*Intentions*

Often we end up doing that which we most tried to avoid. I remember the wife of Ambassador Dwight Morrow telling a story about when her daughters were very small girls.

Mrs. Morrow gave a high tea at which one of the guests was to be J.P. Morgan. The girls were to be brought in, introduced and ushered out. Mrs. Morrow's great fear was the possibility that Anne, the most outspoken, might comment upon Mr. Morgan's bulbous nose. She therefore took pains to explain to Anne that personal observations were impolite, and to caution her especially against making any comment upon Mr. Morgan's nose, no matter what she might think of it. When the moment came and the children were brought in, Mrs. Morrow held her breath as she saw Anne's gaze fix unfalteringly upon this objective and remain there. Nonetheless, the introductions were made, the little girls curtsied and were sent on their way.

With a sigh of relief Mrs. Morrow turned back to her duties as hostess and said to her chief guest, "AND NOW, MR. MORGAN, WILL YOU HAVE CREAM OR LEMON IN YOUR NOSE?"

(And similarly, sometimes the mistake we most try to avoid is the one we end up making. Today it was my intention to give real recognition to one guest, yet this was the one name I failed to introduce . . .)

Government—*Stupidity*

Back in 1960 when Soviet Premier Nikita Khrushchev came to the United Nations, he created quite a stir in the Assembly when, in a heated tirade, he took off his shoe and pounded on the table with it. In the best tradition of British unflappability, Prime Minister Harold Macmillan remarked calmly, "I'D LIKE THAT TRANSLATED, IF I MAY."

(Similarly, I'd like to find out what the government means by their act of . . .)

Overselling—*Audience*

Mrs. Clare Boothe Luce, well-known playwright and wife of the late publisher of *Time,* became a Catholic in middle life and had, of course, all the enthusiasm of the convert. Under President Eisenhower, she was appointed ambassador to Italy, and while she was there, it is said, a reporter once spied her in earnest conversation with the Pope.

It occurred to the reporter that a conversation between Pope and ambassador might have enormous news value, so he drifted closer in an attempt to overhear.

He finally made it, and the first words he heard were those of His Holiness, saying in accented English, "BUT YOU DON'T UNDERSTAND, MRS. LUCE, I ALREADY AM A CATHOLIC."

(Well, are we running the risk of oversell when we . . .)

Arrangements—*Honoree*

In 1940, the Earl of Halifax arrived in Washington as the new ambassador to the United States. In one of his first weeks there he was taken to his first baseball game. Lord Halifax remarked to his host that he could see that baseball was derived from cricket because in both, the batsman tries to hit the ball and advance himself.

In the second inning the Washington batter received four wide pitches. When the player ambled towards first base, the British Earl was befuddled.

"Why is that man not running? He is just strolling towards the base."

"You don't understand—he's got four balls."

"Oh, I see," replied his Lordship. "Running would be difficult for him."

(Well, our friend we honor tonight has no difficulty in running anything.)

Conduct—*Cautious*

The problem with being in the spotlight is that you're constantly under microscopic scrutiny. I find myself sympathetic to Pope John, who told a friend during a diplomatic reception he attended in Rome, "If a woman arrives wearing a gown that is cut daringly low, everybody gazes not at the lady but at me, to see if I'm looking at the lady."

(Similarly, in the delicate situation we find ourselves in, we must go to great lengths not to appear . . .)

Compromise—*Solution*

When former Prime Minister Harold Macmillan was British Resident in Algeria during World War II, he was called upon to settle a dispute between British and American officers in the Allied mess. The Americans wanted alcohol served before meals, the British with their meals.

Macmillan's solution was worthy of Solomon: "Henceforth, we will all drink before meals in deference to the Americans, and we will all drink during dinner in deference to the British."

(Well, in this situation I think we have found a compromise that will satisfy both sides.)

Diplomat—*Honoree*

At a formal White House dinner, Mrs. Grover Cleveland noted that the young State Department aide was staring strangely at his entree. She looked and saw that there was a big bug on top of his asparagus.

Catching the First Lady's glance, the young man speared the stalk with the bug and downed it in a swallow.

Afterwards Mrs. Cleveland whispered to the young man as he left the White House, "ANYONE WHO HAS THE COURAGE AND TACT TO EAT A BUG AS IF IT WERE BERNAISE OUGHT TO BE AN AMBASSADOR."

(That young man, was indeed promoted; and today we salute someone who is also both fearless and yet able to act with finesse . . .)

EMERGENCY WARD

The only way to keep your health is to eat what you don't want, drink what you don't like and do what you'd druther not.

Mark Twain

He is a fool that makes his doctor his heir.

Ben Franklin

When a doctor doesn't know, he calls it a virus, when he does know and can't cure it he calls it an allergy.

From the Humes File

A physician's fees are ill-gotten gains.

From the Humes File

A doctor is a general practitioner who calls in a specialist to share the blame.

From the Humes File

Defiance—*Resistance*

My reaction is somewhat similar to a doctor I heard about recently. He was up in front of the Ethics Committee of the county medical association for using unprofessional language with a patient.

"Fellow doctors," he explained, "I had been up late Saturday night—the night before—in the hospital. So I decided on Sunday afternoon to take a nap. To make sure I was not interrupted, I pulled out the phone plug in the bedroom and then dozed off.

"Sometime later I was wakened by an insistent phone ring which came from downstairs. I waited but it kept ringing. I put on my robe, went downstairs and as I picked the phone up the connection was turned off. I made my way back upstairs. No sooner had I laid down than the phone started ringing again, so wearily I went down the stairs again. I picked up the phone and a woman's voice said, 'DOCTOR, HOW DO YOU USE A RECTAL THERMOMETER.'"

(Well, the doctor's reply is much what I would like to say to . . .)

Profession—*Mix-up*

An eminent heart specialist was attending a conference in Las Vegas. At one reception, he was in animated conversation with a lovely young thing wearing a great deal of makeup and the barest minimum of clothing. It was only a few minutes too late that the good doctor became aware that his wife, whom he thought was safely in the next room, was watching him with a steely glare.

Clearing his throat, the doctor said, "Ah, my dear, that young lady over there and I were just indulging in a purely professional consultation.

"SO I CAN WELL IMAGINE," said his wife icily, "BUT WAS IT YOUR PROFESSION OR HERS?"

Misjudgment—*Misreading*

The psychiatrist polished his glasses and said to his patient, "It will help me understand your problems better if I may set up some free associations. Please answer the following questions with the first thought that comes into your mind.

"What is it that a man does standing, a lady sitting down and a dog on three legs?"

The patient replied, without hesitation, "Shakes hands."

"And what is it that a dog does in the back yard that produces something you would not care to step into unexpectedly?"

The patient said, "Digs a hole."

"WELL, THAT'S WHAT I THOUGHT. YOU OUGHT TO HEAR SOME OF THE ANSWERS I'VE BEEN GETTING."

Expertise—*Audience*

On the *Queen Elizabeth* ocean liner returning from England, actress Zsa Zsa Gabor noted that the passenger next to her on the deck chair was coughing and sneezing with a bad head cold.

"Excuse me," said Zsa Zsa, "but I know just the cure. Have the deck steward brew you a steaming pot of tea and then add some whiskey to it. Trust me—it works," added the actress. "I'm Zsa Zsa Gabor from Beverly Hills. What is your name?"

The elderly man, after thanking her, said, "I'M LOUIS MAYO OF THE MAYO CLINIC IN ROCHESTER, MINNESOTA."

(Well, in the audience I see many of people who know a lot more about this subject than I . . .)

Doctor—*Mistake*

Members of the medical profession get more than their share of criticism. They are often accused of burying their mistakes. I recall the story of the man who died and arrived at the gates of Heaven. A messenger of Saint Peter took his name and disappeared. Later, the messenger came back and told the newly arrived applicant to Heaven that he was very sorry but his name was not on the books. He was not registered to be received in Heaven. The messenger suggested that the man try Hell.

The poor fellow made his way to the gates of Hell and was promptly interviewed by a representative of Satan. Here again he was informed that he was not on the books and not registered to be admitted to Hell. It was suggested that he return to Heaven once more.

The fellow, now thoroughly confused, returned to the pearly gates and announced that his name had not been found on the register in Hell and that Satan had suggested that he try Heaven again. The fellow was taken to the office outside the gates and Saint Peter himself carefully checked every name again. Suddenly, the name was discovered far down the list.

Saint Peter turned to him and said, "THERE SEEMS TO HAVE BEEN A MISTAKE HERE. YOU ARE NOT DUE TO ARRIVE IN HEAVEN FOR SIX MORE YEARS. WHO IS YOUR DOCTOR?"

Problem—*Awareness*

Our situation today is not dissimilar to the case of the man who was so forgetful he drove his friends to distraction. They finally insisted that he see a psychiatrist, which he did.

He said to the psychiatrist, "Doctor, I have this terrible problem with forgetfulness."

The doctor asked, "How long have you had this problem?"

To which the man replied, "WHAT PROBLEM?"

(Tonight we must ask what is the problem facing us . . .)

Perfection—*Honoree*

Words cannot express the true value to the community of the man we honor tonight. It reminds me of some years ago when the sultan of an Arab emirate came to the U.S. for an eye operation. The doctor had no problem performing the operation but he worried about what to charge the royal patient. If he overcharged, it would reflect unfavorably on international relationships and goodwill. On the other hand, if he undercharged, the sultan would feel the operation was not serious enough to require his medical services.

The doctor checked with some of his colleagues and was almost ready to settle for $5,000, until one colleague suggested he consult a lawyer in New York who specialized in middle Eastern affairs. The lawyer recommended that the doctor specify no particular amount but that he submit instead a blank statement with the footnote, "The sultan can do no wrong," and then let the sultan decide what he thought the operation was worth. The doctor followed this advice.

It was not long after that that the doctor actually received a check from the royal exchequer of the sultanate for $75,000. And then it was not long after that the doctor received a blank invoice from the lawyer penned with the footnote, "THE SURGEON CAN DO NO WRONG."

(And while our honoree would modestly disclaim her value, we know that as far as we are concerned, she also can do no wrong.)

Public Relations—*Exaggeration*

The interpretation some of our friends in the press have put on the straightforward recommendations and findings of the committee remind me very much of the young matron who told her husband after a visit with the doctor, "Honey, the doctor said I am in a very distraught condition and that it is essential for me to go to St. Tropez, then to Aspen, and to buy myself a new mink wrap."

The husband immediately called the doctor back. "What did you mean by all this stuff about St. Tropez, Aspen and mink coats?"

"WHAT? I JUST RECOMMENDED TO YOUR WIFE A REGIMEN OF FREQUENT BATHS, PLENTY OF FRESH AIR AND TO BE SURE TO DRESS IN WARM CLOTHES."

(Well, let us cut away some of the verbiage and public relations talk and examine . . .)

Bigotry—*Brotherhood*

The story is told of the grand wizard of the Ku Klux Klan of Alabama, who was ailing. He went to a top doctor in Montgomery.

After the checkup, the doctor called him and said, "I can give you the bad news or the worst news."

"What's the bad news doc?"

"You have a fatal disease."

"Well, what news could be worse than that."

"YOU'RE DYING OF SICKLE CELL ANEMIA."

(Well we are all one race—children of God.)

Knowledge—*Plans*

The befuddled patient called on the doctor. "I just hope it's not Alzheimer's," he said. "Maybe there's some kind of memory medicine you can give me. See, I'm getting terribly forgetful. I lose track of where I'm going or what I'm supposed to do when I get there. What should I do?" he asked glumly.

The doctor promptly suggested, "PAY ME IN ADVANCE."

(Well, we are not asking to be paid in advance but we would like to know in advance what . . .)

Opinion—*Consultant*

Sometimes we go off blindly without carefully thinking out all the options. I recall three college roommates who used to get together regularly over the years even though their professional lives differed widely; one had become an attorney, one a professor of Italian literature and one a zoologist. When next they met, they made a pretty gloomy trio, and it turned out that each had been told by his physician that he had only six months to live. Understandably, the conversation turned to the way in which each intended to live out his remaining days.

"I'm going to Rowanda in Africa," decided the zoologist. "I've always wanted to see the mountain gorilla in its native habitat."

"Italy for me. I want to walk where Dante walked, to be buried near the great man. And you?" asked the professor, turning to the third friend. "What would you like to see?"

The lawyer said, "ANOTHER DOCTOR."

(And similarly I think we would like another opinion on this problem.)

Report—*Good News/Bad News*

Like a lot of reports there is some good news and bad news. I recall the sad story of the poor young fellow who was in a terrible motorcycle accident. When he came out from under the anaesthetic, the doctor was leaning over him sympathetically.

"Son," she said kindly, "I've got to break some terrible news to you, but I have some good news too. The bad news is that you were in a terrible accident and we had to amputate both legs below the knee."

"Oh no," gasped the lad. "What's the good news—I could use it."

"See that fellow in the bed across the aisle? HE'D LIKE TO BUY YOUR BOOTS."

(Well, our good news is a lot better than that . . .)

Honoree—*Faults*

We are happy that our honored guest is enjoying good health, and we can report with absolute confidence that she did not hear this kind of diagnosis when she last went for a check-up. This physical involved a very prim and proper man who went to the doctor for his regular check-up. He said, "I feel terrible. Please examine me and tell me what's wrong."

"Let's begin with a few questions," said the doctor. "Do you drink much?"

"Alcohol?" said the man. "I'm a teetotaler. Never touch a drop."

"How about smoking?" asked the doctor.

"Never," replied the man. "Tobacco is bad and I have strong principles against it."

"Well, uh," asked the doctor, "do you have much of a sex life?"

"Oh, no," said the man. "Sex is sin. I'm in bed by 9:30 every night—always have been."

The doctor paused, looked at the man hard, and asked, "Well, do you have pains in your head?"

"Yes," said the man. "I have terrible pains in my head."

"O.K.," said the doctor, "THAT'S YOUR TROUBLE. YOUR HALO IS TOO TIGHT."

(Well, I can tell you that our honoree has not been having any headaches.)

Analysis—*Interpretation*

The trends out there lend themselves to different interpretations. I remember hearing from an analyst who was concerned about the results of a Rorschach test he had just given to a patient who associated every ink blot with some sort of sexual activity.

"I want to study the results of your test over the weekend and then see you again on Monday," he said to the patient.

"OKAY, DOCTOR. BY THE WAY, I'M GOING TO A STAG PARTY TOMORROW NIGHT. ANY CHANCE I MIGHT BORROW THOSE DIRTY PICTURES OF YOURS?"

Situation—*Advantage*

The situation out there is ready to be taken advantage of. It reminds me of the case of a beautiful woman who had a problem with drink. She went to a psychiatrist.

"It's liquor, doctor. Whenever I have a few drinks I have a compulsion to make love to whomever I happen to be with."

"I see," said the doctor. "WELL, SUPPOSE I JUST MIX US UP A COUPLE OF COCKTAILS, THEN YOU AND I SIT DOWN NICE AND RELAXED AND DISCUSS THIS COMPULSIVE NEUROSIS OF YOURS."

EXECUTIVE SUITE

It is not the crook in modern business we have to fear, but the honest man who doesn't know what he is doing.

Owen D. Young

A verbal contract isn't worth the paper it is printed on.

Samuel Goldwyn

A banker is a fellow who lends his umbrella when the sun is shining and wants it back the minute it begins to rain.

From the Humes File

The feminists say we executives want a secretary to take things down and a wife to pick things up.

From the Humes File

A businessman can't win these days; if he does something wrong he's fined; if he does something right he's taxed.

From the Humes File

A man is known by the company that keeps him.

From the Humes File

Sales—*Drive*

A small business was in trouble with its sales. The sales manager decided to call in an expert to give her an outsider's viewpoint. After she had gone over his plans and problems, the sales manager took the expert to a map on the wall and showed him brightly colored pins stuck wherever he had a sales respresentative.

"Now," she asked the expert, "for a starter, what is the first thing we should do?"

"WELL," replied the expert, "THE FIRST THING IS TO TAKE THOSE PINS OUT OF THE MAP AND STICK THEM INTO SALES REPS."

(But one thing we don't have to do is put pins into our sales force . . .)

Profit—*Retail*

I am always happy to have the chance to speak to a group of business people such as yourselves, because it is business that powers America. It provides the jobs, builds the homes, and expands the economy. The profit motive is not something to condemn but to commend.

In that connection I recall a college reunion I attended not long ago. One grad who was remembered as the dimmest in the class returned in a chauffeured Rolls-Royce. It seems he had become a fabulously successful president of a gasket company. Naturally all of us, his former classmates, were curious how one that stupid had made so much money. So after we plied him with lots of drinks, a friend of mine put the question to him, "Just how were you able to put together this gasket operation you run?"

"IT WAS EASY," he replied. "I FOUND A MANUFACTURER WHO COULD MAKE THEM AT ONE CENT APIECE AND THEN I SOLD THEM AT FIVE CENTS APIECE. AND YOU JUST CAN'T BEAT THAT FOUR PERCENT PROFIT."

Procedure—*Rules*

Two executives were talking about the smashing new receptionist they had hired.

The older man said, "The first thing we have to do is to teach her what's right and wrong."

"YEAH," said the young man leering. "WE'LL SPLIT IT UP—YOU BE THE ONE TO TEACH HER WHAT'S RIGHT AND I'LL . . ."

(Well, we do have some do's and don'ts in the way we operate.)

Resources—*Capital*

No matter how strong our intentions are or how great our ideas we still have to possess the necessary resources. I remember attending a testimonial dinner for a town's leading citizen. He had come to the city as young man and the story was that he had come with only the shirt on his back and a bundle tied in a red bandanna.

Now this man was the president of the biggest bank and the city's biggest office building was named after him. He lived in a mansion with a swimming pool and tennis courts.

At the end of the banquet honoring this man a new reporter in town raised his hand in the back and asked timidly, "Sir, when you walked into this town thirty years ago, could you tell me what you had wrapped in that red bandanna?"

"I THINK, SON," he said, "I WAS CARRYING ABOUT $100,000 IN CASH AND SOME $100,000 IN GOVERNMENT BONDS."

(Well, the point is no matter how brilliant the idea or how sound the management or leadership you still have to have the capital investment.)

Repeat—*Rejection*

Although I have given more than a few speeches, this is one of the few times a group has had me back again. Some organizations, like people, often don't want a thing a second time.

For example, a head of an American company not long ago was visiting his London office. He arrived on one of those typical foggy London nights and went to a club which had a reciprocal membership with his club in Houston. Hoping to strike up a conversation with a distinguished-looking Englishman sitting nearby, he said, "May I buy you a drink?"

"No," said the Britisher coolly. "Don't drink. Tried alcohol once and didn't like it. Thank you anyway."

My friend ordered himself a drink and after a while he thought he'd try to make conversation again, so he said, "Would you like one of my cigars?"

"No. Don't smoke. Tried tobacco once and didn't like it. Thank you anyway."

That stopped my friend, but then after a bit he thought,

surely the gentleman would not be adverse to playing some rummy, so he asked him to join him in a game.

"No. Don't like card games. Tried it once and didn't like it. But my son will be dropping by after a bit. Perhaps he'll join you."

My American friend settled back in his chair and said, "YOUR ONLY SON, I RECKON!"

(I'm glad you had the tolerance and fortitude to try me a second time . . .)

FAMILY ROOM

Before I got married, I had six theories about bringing up children. Now I have six children and no theories.

John Wilmot, Earl of Rochester

Youth is a wonderful thing. What a crime to waste it on children.

George Bernard Shaw

The first half of our life is ruined by our parents and the second half by our children.

Clarence Darrow

It now costs more to amuse a child than it did once to educate either of his parents.

From the Humes File

The family that stays together probably has only one car.

From the Humes File

Urgency—*Action*

My cousin has a teenage daughter who felt she had the right to do anything she pleased with her own room, and yet who was very conscious of the importance of making a better world. One day she was called downstairs by her parents.

"Yeah, what is it now?" she asked.

"It's your room," replied her parents.

"I know it's my room," she replied, "and I have a right to keep it the way I want to."

"But," said her mother, "when anyone opens the door, things spill out into the hall, and the air coming out under the door doesn't smell very good."

"Well, so what are you going to do about it? I'm pretty busy with my work," said the girl.

Her father replied, "We're going to give you a choice. EITHER CLEAN UP YOUR ROOM OR FILE AN ENVIRONMENTAL IMPACT STATEMENT."

(Well, we are going to have to clean up our act if we . . .)

HALLS OF IVY

There is nothing so stupid as an educated man, if you get him off the thing he was educated on.

Will Rogers

I find the three major administrative problems on a campus are sex for students, athletics for alumni and parking for the faculty.

Clark Kerr,
President, U.C.L.A

Those who go to college and never get out are called professors.

From the Humes File

Scholarship is the attempt to exhaust a subject by first exhausting the reader.

From the Humes File

Some go to college to learn to think but most go to college to learn what the professor's think.

From the Humes File

In every college there are some students who mistake a liberal education with a generous allowance.

From the Humes File

Professional—*Experts*

Four Harvard English professors, on a walk in Boston's "Combat Zone," encountered a group of ladies clearly of that class described as being "of easy virtue."

"Ah," said one of the scholars, "a jam of tarts."

"Not at all," said the second, "say, rather, a flourish of strumpets."

"Or," said the third, "an essay of Trollope's."

And the fourth said, "RATHER, I THINK, AN ANTHOLOGY OF PROS."

(Well, I see in the audience tonight an assembly of professionals in various fields.)

Stupidity—*Mess*

A Texan walked into the offices of the president of a small Texas college and said, "I would like to donate a million dollars tax free to this institution."

The president's eyes opened wide and he said, "That is a kindly notion, sir. We will be pleased to accept it."

"There's a condition. I would like to have an honorary degree."

"No problem," said the president. "That can be arranged."

"For my horse," said the Texan.

Now the president got to his feet in shock. "For your horse?"

"Yes, my mare, Betsy. She's carried me for many years and I owe her a lot. I would like to have her receive a Tr.D., a Doctor of Transportation."

"But we can't give an honorary degree to a horse."

"I'm sorry to hear you say so, because in that case I can't give you a million dollars."

"Well, wait a minute," said the president, sweating profusely. "Let me consult the board of trustees."

The board was convened in a hurry and listened to the story in various grades of shock and disbelief, all except the oldest trustee, whose eyes were closed and who seemed asleep.

The old trustee listened to the president, who said, "We can't give a horse an honorary degree, no matter how much money is involved."

At this point, the oldest trustee opened his eyes and said, "For Heaven's sake, take the money and give the horse his degree."

Said the president, "Don't you think that would be a disgrace to us?"

"WELL," replied the oldest trustee, "FOR YEARS WE'VE BEEN GIVING OUT DEGREES TO PART OF A HORSE—WE MIGHT AS WELL GIVE A DEGREE TO A WHOLE ONE!"

(And speaking of horse's ass ideas, we . . .)

Preparation—*Unprepared*

William Lyon Phelps, a professor of English at Yale, gave an examination on English literature just before Christmas. One student handed in a very short paper, reading, "Only God knows the answer to this question. Merry Christmas!" Phelps returned the paper after Christmas vacation with this note: "GOD GETS AN A. YOU GET AN F. HAPPY NEW YEAR!"

(We all have our assignments before us—and we'd better be fully prepared.)

Expert—*Authority*

Sometimes I think we have a tendency to put a halo around those young people who are fortunate enough to make it into some highly respected college or university.

Recently, I was visiting a friend in Cambridge, Massachusetts, home of several well-known institutions of higher learning. I accompanied my friend to the supermarket on Saturday, and while we were in line, I saw a young college student wheel a heavily laden cart up to a cash register that was clearly marked, "This line is for people with one to six items only."

The young girl at the cash register looked at the loaded cart, turned to the boy who was helping her bag groceries, and said, "THAT GUY EITHER GOES TO HARVARD AND CAN'T COUNT—OR TO M.I.T. AND CAN'T READ!"

(Well, today we have an authority who has the requisite experience in the field. She can count and knows how to read the bottom line.)

Age—*Service*

When Professor Zephaniah Stewart retired from active service as head of the classics department at Harvard, someone commented on his new title of Professor Emeritus.

"You know what that means?" replied Professor Stewart. "'E' COMES FROM THE LATIN MEANING 'OUT,' AND 'MERITUS' MEANS 'OUGHT TO BE.'"

(Well, at sixty-four I ought to be out, but fortunately I am allowed to continue on . . .)

Analysis—*Problem*

Back in college I remember a story our professor told us about three young women who were attending a class in logic. The professor stated he was going to test their ability at situation reasoning.

"Let us assume," he said, "that you are aboard a small craft alone in the Pacific and you spot a vessel approaching you with several thousand sex-starved sailors on board. What would you do in this situation to avoid any problem?"

"I would attempt to turn my craft in the opposite direction," said the redhead.

"I would pass them trusting my knife to keep me safe," said the brunette.

"FRANKLY," murmured the blonde beauty, "I UNDERSTAND THE SITUATION, BUT I FAIL TO SEE THE PROBLEM."

(Similarly, I don't see as a problem the situation . . .)

HOMETOWN

There isn't much to be seen in a little town, but what you hear makes up for it.

Frank Hubbard

Love your neighbor but don't pull down your hedge.

Thomas Fuller

A neighborhood is where, when you go out of it, you get beat up.

From the Humes File

There is no place like home and many a man is glad of it.

From the Humes File

Overselling—*Sales*

My mother told me about a problem that occurred in her neighborhood when she was growing up in Pittsburgh. A young, red-haired, Irish women had fallen in love with Alec.

As she described her young swain to her mother, she began to sob.

"Why are you crying?"

"Because he is a Presbyterian." The young woman began to weep uncontrollably.

"Now wait, Kathy," said her mother. "Why not try some real salesmanship? Tell him how wonderful our church is. We're the first Christian church. Or tell him of our great beliefs, our martyrs, our saints, the marvelous service the Church has done for the world, the marvelous cathedrals and chapels, the promise of salvation, and the wonderful comfort and inspiration given by our priests through their words and their listening to our confessions and forgiving us our sins. You know all this. Go out and sell Alec on the Church!"

Katherine dried her eyes and agreed to try. She had a number of dates with Alec and for a while was looking happier. But one evening after a date her mother heard her sobbing again. "What's the matter, darling?" asked Kathy's mother. "Didn't it work?"

"NO, MOTHER, NO!" sobbed Katherine. "I OVERSOLD HIM. HE WANTS TO BECOME A PRIEST."

Help—*Assistance*

A successful conclusion to my talk tonight depends not on me but on you. But I know you have the concern, compassion and commitment to do it. None of you could be characterized as being like the three brothers I recently heard about. They were the children of a hard-working couple back home who had struggled for thirty years, sacrificing themselves for their three sons whom they put through college. Never once did they take a vacation. Now they wanted to take a trip to Florida and they asked their sons for some money.

The first son was a lawyer, and he said, "No, I can't do it. I'm just fitting out a new law office and sending my son to an expensive camp."

So they asked their second son, a doctor. But he said, "No, I'm sorry I can't. I've just bought a new house and my wife and I are putting in a new kitchen."

Then they asked the third son, who was an engineer. He replied, "It's impossible for me to do it. I just bought a big boat for the family and we are remodeling our summer home on the lake."

Finally the father pleaded, "Look, we have worked all our lives without one day of vacation. We never saved any money except for your education. In fact, do you realize that your mother and I were so busy working trying to save money that we never took the time out to get a marriage license?"

"Father," said all three sons in unison, "Do you realize what that makes us?"

"YES," said the father, "AND CHEAP ONES, TOO."

(But I know we have no *cheap* ones in the audience tonight . . .)

Bureaucracy—*Regulations*

Back in my hometown there was a Scoutmaster who expected the members of his troop to report at least one good deed that they had done in the previous week.

One evening three of his members arrived late. He asked what were their good deeds.

The first youth replied, "Helping an old lady across the street." The Scoutmaster expressed his approval and looked at the second Scout. He likewise reported that he, too, had assisted an old lady across the street. The Scoutmaster again nodded his assent and then he looked at the third Scout, who also said that he had helped an old lady across the street.

"What?" exclaimed the Scoutmaster, "You all helped old ladies across the street?"

"No," they answered. "It was just one lady and all three of us helped."

"It took three of you to help the lady?"

"WELL, IT DOES WHEN SHE DIDN'T WANT TO GO!"

(Well, that describes our position with the government. They say "We're here to help you" but we don't want their help, particularly when it makes our economic growth go in the wrong direction.)

Miracles—*Improvements*

We expect some improvement but we are not miracle makers. I am reminded of the man of the house who came home and his wife asked him to repair the broken dryer.

"Who do you think I am, Mr. Fixit?"

The next day, when he came home, she asked him to fix the washing machine.

"Who do you think I am," he replied, "Mr. Maytag?"

The next night when he returned, his wife informed him that the washing machine and dryer had been fixed.

"Who did it?" he asked.

"The milkman."

"What did you pay him?"

"Well he said he wanted either a cake baked for him or to sleep with me."

"What kind of cake did you bake for him?"

"WHO DO YOU THINK I AM," she replied, "BETTY CROCKER?"

(Well, we are not miracle workers . . .)

Urgency—*Problem*

We are faced with an immediate problem that will not wait another couple of years. I am reminded of a certain funeral, where a husband was beside himself with grief and distraction at the death of his wife. His loud weeping as the coffin was lowered into the grave impressed the bystanders and one of them was moved to make an attempt at consolation.

"Tony, Tony," he said, patting the widower's shoulder in gentle commiseration, "it seems terrible now, but time is a great healer. Why, in a year or two you'll even be dating other women."

Tony pushed aside the other's arm roughly. "A YEAR YOU SAY!" he cried furiously. "WHAT AM I GOING TO DO TONIGHT?"

Friends—*Support*

Over the past few years, I know of no group that has been more of a staunch friend than your organization. You have been there in the pinch, when really needed. Of course, as I learned first as a Boy Scout, that's when you really need friends.

The Scoutmaster had taken a group of us out for our first overnight hike. Since there were lots of copperhead snakes in the region, the Scoutmaster gave us these instructions: "If any of you are bitten by a snake, immediately apply your mouth to the puncture and suck vigorously at the aperture."

At this point, one of my fellow Scouts said, "What happens, sir, if you get bitten on the backside?"

The Scoutmaster thought for a moment and then told us: "IT'S THEN THAT YOU GET TO KNOW YOUR REAL FRIENDS."

(In a different way, I have come to know what a real friend your organization has been . . .)

Support—*Organization*

I have always had high respect for your organization and the work that it has been doing. I might say that my admiration for you is like what a gas-meter man in my town said not long ago under different circumstances.

A neighbor of mine, on her day off, decided to get some household chores done. Still dressed in her housecoat, she spied above the washing machine in the basement a big spider in a cobweb. She grabbed the nearest means of protection—her son's football helmet—and with a baseball bat she slew the beast. Needing something to wrap up the remains, she took off her housecoat, scooped up the web and popped it in one motion into the washing machine. At that moment, the meter man appeared, looked at the woman in her altogether, with the baseball bat and football helmet, and said. "LADY, I DON'T KNOW WHAT SPORT YOU'RE TRYING TO PLAY, BUT WHATEVER IT IS I'M SURE ROOTING FOR YOUR TEAM."

(And knowing the great activities your society is actively engaged in, I am sure rooting for the success . . .)

Freedom—*Complaint*

A neighbor down the street emigrated from Moscow some years ago. On his aged grandmother's 85th birthday, he called her and during the conversation got to speak to his cousin.

"How are things, Dmitri?"

"Oh, I just got into a four-room apartment for me and my family. But many still are with their parents or are in two-room flats, so I can't complain."

"How's the food situation?"

"Well, we can now buy some fresh meat and vegetables so even if we have to stand in line for an hour I can't complain."

"How do you get around?"

"I still use my bike, but I'm on the short two-year waiting list for a Ziti auto—I can't complain. How about yourself?"

"Well, we have a split-level house with a pool here, a supermarket full of every kind of fruit and fresh vegetables and a butcher's department stocked with all kinds of beef. It's twenty blocks away but that's no problem with my new luxury automobile. WHAT'S MORE I CAN COMPLAIN."

(Well, in America we are free to criticize . . .)

Donor—Involvement

I remember once in a hospital fundraising drive the chairman of the campaign decided to call personally at the home of the town's wealthiest citizen, a man well known for his tightness with a dollar. Remarking on the impressive economic resources of his host, the committee chairman pointed out how miserly it would seem if the town's richest man failed to give a substantial donation to the annual charity drive.

"Since you've gone to so much trouble checking on my assets," the millionaire retorted, "let me fill you in on some facts you may have overlooked. I have a ninety-one-year-old mother who has been hospitalized for the past five years, a widowed daughter with five young children and no means of support, and two brothers who owe the government a fortune in back taxes. Now, I think you'll agree, young man, that charity begins at home."

Ashamed for having misjudged his host, the fundraiser apologized for his tactlessness and added, "I had no idea you were saddled with so many family debts."

"I'M NOT," replied the millionaire, "BUT YOU MUST BE CRAZY TO THINK I'D GIVE MONEY TO STRANGERS WHEN I WON'T EVEN HELP MY OWN RELATIVES."

(Fortunately, our drive is distinguished by many who are not lacking a spirit of humanity and in fact are singularly generous.)

Seller's Market—*Offer*

It's a seller's market out there if you have a service that's in demand. I remember hearing a story about a young man in the town I grew up in. This nervous young man was rushing into a drugstore, obviously embarrassed when a prim, middle-aged woman asked if she could serve him.

"No-no," he stammered, "I'd rather see the druggist."

"I'm the pharmacist," she responded cheerfully. "What can I do for you?"

"Oh . . . well, uh, it's nothing important," he said, and turned to leave.

"Young man," said the woman, "my sister and I have been running this drugstore for nearly thirty years. There is nothing you can tell us that will embarrass us."

"Well, all right," he said. "I have this awful sexual hunger that nothing will appease. No matter how many times I make love, I still want to make love again. Is there anything you can give me for it?"

"Just a moment," said the little lady, "I'll have to discuss this with my sister."

A few minutes later she returned. "THE BEST WE CAN OFFER," she said, "IS $200 A WEEK AND HALF-INTEREST IN THE BUSINESS."

LOCKER ROOM

I do not think winning is the most important thing—it's the only thing.

Vince Lombardi

Nice guys finish last.

Leo Durocher

Games are for people who can neither read nor think.

George Bernard Shaw

Although he is a poor fielder, he is also a very poor hitter.

Ring Lardner

Some players are good losers, while others don't pretend.

From the Humes File

If at first you don't succeed, try second base.

From the Humes File

Baseball is the only place in life where a sacrifice is really appreciated.

From the Humes File

A football game is where the spectators have four quarters to finish a fifth.

From the Humes File

The toughest problems a football coach has to face are defensive linebackers and offensive alumni.

From the Humes File

Challenge—*Competition*

In this challenging situation our very manhood is being tested. It is like the time the Alabama football team was behind three touchdowns at half-time. Their coach, Bear Bryant, addressed the team in the locker room just before the second half, "WELL, GIRLS, SHALL WE GO?" The Crimson Tide with their manhood challenged went out and won the game.

(Well, the competition has given us a challenge . . .)

Analysis—*Perspective*

Bear Bryant, Alabama's great football coach, once kept a big lummox on the squad all season in the vain hope that he could teach him the fundamentals of blocking and tackling. His varsity line averaged 180 pounds; the lummox weighed 250. "All that beef going to waste," Bryant would moan. But the lummox, though patient, willing and eager to please, simply couldn't learn.

In a skull session before the season's final game with Clemson, Bryant suddenly pointed at the lummox and demanded, "You, there! What would you do if we had the ball on their five-yard line, fourth down and thirty seconds left to play—with Alabama trailing by two points?"

The lummox pondered briefly, and then answered, "I'D MOVE DOWN TO THE END OF THE BENCH, MR. BRYANT, SO I COULD SEE BETTER."

(Well, I am sure our next speaker with his perspective will bring valuable insights . . .)

Facts—*Detail*

When Mets telecaster Ralph Kiner was a National League home run king for the Pirates, he was married to tennis star Nancy Chafee.

A reporter asked if he could beat her at tennis and Kiner answered, "As a matter of fact, I just did two weeks ago."

"What was the score?"

Kiner answered, "4–6, 10–8, 18–16."

"How did you do that?" asked the reporter skeptically. "Wasn't she well?"

"PERFECTLY WELL," came Kiner's indignant response. "EXCEPT FOR THE FACT THAT SHE WAS EIGHT MONTHS PREGNANT."

(Well, sometimes little facts are the most important.)

Logic—*Fallacious*

When the hard-drinking Hack Wilson was slugging for the Brooklyn Dodgers, his abstemious manager Max Carey called a meeting for the entire team. Although Wilson was hitting .300 for the Dodgers and pumping out homers, he had to be saved somehow from himself! So Carey tried the psychological approach: health, doctors' warnings and all that. As he called the players' meeting to order, Max stood on a table on which he had placed two glasses and a plate of live wiggleworms. One glass was filled with water, the other with gin, Wilson's favorite elixir. With a flourish, the manager dropped a worm in the glass of water. It wriggled happily. Now Max plunged the same worm into the gin: it stiffened and expired. A murmur ran through the room and some of the players were obviously impressed. Not Wilson. Hack didn't even seem interested. Manager Carey waited a little, hoping for some delayed reaction from his wayward member. When none came, he prodded, "That mean anything to you, Wilson?"

"Sure, Skipper," answered Hack, "IT PROVES IF YOU DRINK GIN YOU'LL NEVER HAVE NO WORMS!"

(The same kind of logic characterizes the arguments of our friends. They say . . .)

Age—*Youth*

I recall the 1978 baseball season, which produced only very few .300 hitters in either league. The radio show, *Monitor*, interviewed Ted Williams while he was fishing on the Florida coast. When Ted was asked by a reporter what he thought his batting average would be when one had to consider all the changes in baseball since Williams had retired—airplane travel, artificial turf, specialist relievers and night games—Williams said modestly, "Oh, I guess I would hit about .295." "What, only 295?" asked one of his audience. "DON'T FORGET, YOUNG MAN," said Williams, "COME MARCH, I'LL BE FIFTY-EIGHT YEARS OLD."

(But seriously, I don't think, even with the advantages of youth, I could do as well . . .)

Memory—*Nostalgia*

When Sandy Koufax, the almost unhittable pitcher with a record E.R.A., was approached by a young sports reporter, he answered all the eager lad's questions willingly. "Just one more, Sandy," said the young reporter finally. "What was your favorite pitch when you had the bases full behind you?"

"MY BOY," Koufax replied with a perfectly straight face, "I DON'T RECALL EVER HAVING TO PITCH WITH THE BASES FULL."

(Like Sandy Koufax, some of us, in looking back, tend to forget the rough spots . . .)

Honoree—*Generosity*

One afternoon, in St. Louis, Stan ("The Man") Musial was having a field day against the Chicago pitcher, crusty Bobo Newsom. Stan first slammed a single, then a triple, and then a homer. When Stan came up to bat for the fourth time, the Chicago manager, Charlie Grimm, decided to yank Bobo and take a chance on a rookie relief pitcher. The rookie trudged in from the bullpen and took the ball from Bobo. "Say," he murmured, "has this guy Musial got any weaknesses?" "YEAH," grunted Bobo, "HE CAN'T HIT DOUBLES."

(And if our friend has any weakness it is that he can't say no to someone in need, or hit anyone when he is down . . .)

Arrangements—*Planning*

Muhammad Ali held the heavyweight boxing title for a total of thirteen years over a sixteen-year stretch. During his reign, he was known for the verbal jousting he subjected his opponents to before each bout.

Ali went to see the movie *Rocky II*, which, like its predecessor, featured a boxer modeled pretty closely on Ali. In one scene, this character jeers at Rocky and announces, "I'll destroy you. I am the master of disaster."

After watching the film, Ali said, "MASTER OF DISASTER. WHY DIDN'T I THINK OF THAT!"

(In organizing and planning this meeting anyone but our chairman would have been a "master of disaster." I noticed he has been a master of perfection . . .)

Almost—*Incorrect*

Los Angeles Dodger Don Sutton was one of those pitchers who are constantly under suspicion of illegally doctoring the ball to gain an advantage over the hitters. Like many other pitchers, Sutton did little to discourage such suspicion, reasoning that if hitters are worried about a spitball, the pitcher already has the necessary advantage.

In the middle of one game, the home-plate umpire walked out to the mound and demanded to see Sutton's glove, expecting to find some illegal substance hidden inside. Sutton handed over the glove. Inside, the umpire found a note that read, "YOU'RE GETTING WARM, BUT IT'S NOT HERE."

(Well, the proposal we have heard may be on the right track but it's not quite right.)

Statistics—*Mistake*

As a baseball player, a coach, and a manager, Frankie Frisch never hid his lack of affection for umpires. Once, when Frisch was coaching third base, umpire Bill Klem called a runner out on a close play. Frisch put his hand to his heart and fell to the ground.

Klem calmly walked over to the fallen coach, who lay on the ground with his eyes closed. "FRISCH," Klem said, "DEAD OR ALIVE, YOU'RE OUT OF THE GAME."

(Well, these statistics are not "ballpark figures"; they should be ejected for being dead wrong.)

Action—*Priority*

In 1957, the Milwaukee Braves met the New York Yankees in the World Series. One of the Braves' most fearsome hitters was Henry Aaron, who would go on to become the all-time home run leader in major league history. When he came up to bat, Yankee catcher Yogi Berra did what catchers often do with good hitters—he tried to rattle him. "You're holding the bat the wrong way," Berra said. "Turn it around so you can see the trademark."

With his eyes steady on the pitcher, Aaron said, "DIDN'T COME UP HERE TO READ. CAME UP HERE TO HIT."

(Well, the time for stories is past, it is time to act . . .)

Contributions—*Request*

A star forward was in his senior year at a college with a shady reputation. He was the leading point maker on the basketball team, which was being investigated by half a dozen state and national organizations. Yet the coach was worried about him, because he had recently been trailing off in his basket totals.

"What's troubling him?" he asked his assistant. "His mind always seems to be somewhere else."

"IT'S HIS FAMILY," the assistant explained, "HIS FATHER KEEPS WRITING TO ASK FOR MONEY."

(Similarly, we need your contributions today.)

Birthday—*Excellence*

During the years when Stengel was their manager, the Mets were the laughingstock of the National League. The player who best exemplified the team's hopelessness was Marv Throneberry, known to the Mets' adoring fans as "Marvelous Marv." Throneberry could be relied on to strike out in any key situation and to make an error just when the opposing team needed it most.

One day, the team held a birthday party for manager Casey Stengel, complete with an enormous birthday cake. Throneberry complained, "How come nobody gave me a cake on my birthday?"

"WE WOULD HAVE," Casey said, "BUT WE WERE AFRAID YOU'D DROP IT."

(Today we honor someone who has never dropped the ball.)

Change—*Beating*

Joe Garagiola tells this story about a day he was catching for the St. Louis Cardinals at Wrigley Field in Chicago. One of the distinguishing features of Wrigley is the ivy that covers the outfield walls. Another is the unpredictable wind, which can create nightmares for even the best of pitchers. On this day, the wind was working very much in the batters' favor and the Cubs' pitcher was taking a pounding.

Chicago manager Phil Cavaretta walked slowly to the mound, then took the ball from his pitcher. "I HATE TO TAKE YOU OUT," he said consolingly, "BUT THE OUTFIELDERS ARE GETTING POISON IVY."

(Well, we are taking a beating from all sides . . .)

Problem—*Impasse*

Bronko Nagurski of the Chicago Bears was one of the biggest and strongest men ever to play professional football. On one play from the one-yard line, Nagurski plowed through the defensive line with so much power that he kept going through the end zone. With his head still down, he crashed into a mounted policeman, felling both the cop and his horse, and then plowed into a stadium wall.

Not aware of what he'd just done, Nagurski stood up, cleared his head and said, "THAT LAST MAN SURE HIT ME AWFUL HARD."

(Well, we have run into a stone wall ourselves.)

Statistics—*Sales*

In 1992, Tommy Lasorda's L.A. Dodgers were fighting to stay out of last place. A reporter in September said, "Tommy, I figured out the magic number for you to win the pennant. Know what it is?"

Lasorda muttered. "I KNOW WHAT IT IS—911!"

(Well, the magic number for us in sales is . . .)

Support—*Help*

When journeyman pitcher Bobo Newsom was playing for the hapless Washington Senators in the 1940s, he found himself one day slammed by the Philadelphia A's batters. With the bench and relief pitchers having been depleted by losses earlier in the week, Newsom was not taken out. In the seventh inning, the A's had a comfortable 15–0 lead and Bobo came back to the dugout wearing a disgusted look on his broad face. "What's eating you, Bobo?" asked someone on the bench. "What do you think?" snorted the angry Newsom as he flung his glove aside. "HOW CAN A GUY WIN BALL GAMES WITH THIS LOUSY CLUB IF THEY DON'T GIVE HIM ANY RUNS?"

(Well, I can't say that I wasn't given good support . . .)

Potential—*Future*

In St. Petersburg, Florida where the Yankees trained, a scout rushed up to Casey Stengel and said:

"What do you think of that young outfielder you just signed."

"I FIGGER," said Casey, "THAT HERE A 19-YEAR-OLD PROSPECT HAS A GOOD CHANCE IN 10 YEARS TO TURN 29."

(Similarly, I see little future in this area of the market . . .)

Halfway—*Opportunity*

An investment banker in one of the top blue-chip firms in New York was about to travel to England for several weeks to complete some negotiations.

An avid golfer, the banker called an English acquaintance to ask where he could play some golf.

"Old boy, I'll give you a letter to my club," his friend told him. "It's the Royal Golf Club in Sandwich. It's a unique course by the sea and very exclusive. That's where the Prince of Wales used to play. Just take my letter to the club secretary. They'll ask a few questions and that'll be it."

One bright Saturday morning the New York banker rose early and in his rented Bentley drove out to the club.

The club secretary pulled out his reading glasses, put the half-spectacles on the lower end of his nose, looked down at the application form and asked, "Your father's name?"

"Hamilton Finch Vanderbilt III."

He nodded. "Your mother's?" he asked.

"Alexandra Stuyvesant."

"Your school?"

"St. Paul's, Magna Cum Laude."

"Your university?"

"Princeton, Phi Beta Kappa in English."

"Hmmm," he muttered. "No military service?"

"Yes, in Vietnam, Captain in the Marines."

"Decorations?"

"Distinguished Service Cross Medal."

"Golfing experience?"

"Captain, Princeton team, 1970, and winner, Piping Rock Club Singles, 1975."

"I SEE . . . I SUPPOSE YOU DO QUALIFY FOR A GUEST CARD . . . BUT MIND YOU, IT'S ONLY FOR NINE HOLES."

(Well, in this new market we're not yet established but we are halfway in the door.)

Market—*Demand*

When the Yankees had finished a game against the Twins, Whitey Ford suggested they go to Charlie's, a popular restaurant in Minneapolis.

"NAW," countered Yogi Berra. "NO ONE GOES THERE ANY-MORE BECAUSE IT'S TOO CROWDED."

(Well, the demand is out there . . .)

Truth—*Facts*

When Yogi Berra was coaching for the Mets, Ron Swoboda hit a ball that cleared the wall and bounced back. The umpire called a ground-rule double, saying that it had hit the concrete wall in left field.

Berra argued strenuously that the ball had hit the wooden seats in the stands.

After a heated argument Berra was ejected. His parting shot to the umpire was, "ANYONE WHO CAN'T TELL THE DIF-

FERENCE BETWEEN A BALL HITTING CONCRETE AND ONE HIT-
TING WOOD IS BLIND."

(Well, anyone who can't see or hear what's been happening . . .)

Consumer—*Products*

When Yogi Berra was showed the low attendance records of
the Mets, he remarked, "WHEN PEOPLE DON'T WANT TO
COME OUT TO THE PARK, IT'S HARD TO STOP THEM."

(Well, you can't force consumers to buy a product they
don't like.)

Rut—*Slump*

Yogi Berra was suffering through one of the few slumps in
his magnificent Yankee career. A reporter asked what was
his problem, and Yogi replied, "I'M IN A RUT AND I CAN'T
BREAK THE HABIT."

(It may sound redundant, but we all know what it's like to
be in a pattern that we can't find our way out of . . .)

MADISON AVENUE

You can tell the ideals of a nation by its advertising.

Norman Douglas

Advertising is usually a trick to get you to spend money by
telling you how much you can save. An advertisement is 85
percent confusion and 15 percent commission.

Fred Allen

If I had to do it over again a profession I would have tried is
advertising.

Franklin Roosevelt

The consumer is not a moron; she is your wife.

David Ogilvy

Samson had the right idea about advertising. He took two columns and brought down the house.

From the Humes File

Advertising has made America great, but then advertising makes everything look great.

From the Humes File

Clients—*Competition*

Advertising has always been something of a cutthroat business. Two Madison Avenue advertising men were chatting over a liquid lunch. It seems that an acquaintance of theirs had just gone to the Great Big Agency in the Sky.

"Did you hear about Mark Stone?" asked one of the ad men. "He died last night."

"Good Lord," said the other. "What did he have?"

"A TOOTHPASTE, AN ASPIRIN COMPANY, A COUPLE OF HOTELS, BUT NOTHING WORTH GOING AFTER."

(Seriously, we have picked up a lot of clients in the last year . . .)

Promotion—*Results*

We are hearing some great ideas, but will they get results? I recall the case of a single woman who had been married three times but had never been divorced. The reason she gave is that all of her marriages had been annulled because they hadn't been consummated.

"My first husband was a charming alcoholic and by bedtime he'd be dead to the world. My second husband was quite handsome but on our wedding night I discovered he was more attracted to my brother than me. My third husband, the advertising executive, was a persuasive fellow, but he turned out to be a complete captive of his craft."

"What do you mean?" asked her friend.

"WELL," she said, "HE WOULD SPEND THE WHOLE NIGHT TELLING ME HOW GREAT IT WAS GOING TO BE."

Marketing—*Targeting*

Marketing is a very tricky business. Sometimes the wrong people are targeted. For example, a few months ago in the midst of the airline price wars, the publicity department of one of the airlines introduced a special half-fare for wives accompanying their husbands on trips.

Anticipating some valuable testimonials, the publicity department sent out letters to all wives of businessmen who used the special rates asking how they had enjoyed their trip.

Responses are still pouring in asking, "WHAT TRIP?"

Attention—*Message*

In advertising the success is not only targeting the right audience, but making sure your audience reads the message. A Madison Avenue friend of mine tells of a client who wanted to get his "message" to every married woman in a specific community.

The solution to the problem was simple, according to this enterprising publicist: "WE JUST ADDRESSED LETTERS TO EVERY MARRIED MAN IN TOWN, AND MARKED THEM PERSONAL."

OVAL AND OTHER OFFICES

I never have been hurt by anything I didn't say.

Calvin Coolidge

Whenever a man casts a longing eye in office, a rottenness begins in his conduct.

Thomas Jefferson

I know when things don't go well, they like to blame the President and that is one of the things Presidents are paid for.

John F. Kennedy

Washington is power, then the access to power and ultimately the illusion of access to power.

Alice Roosevelt Longworth, to author

You know it's an election year. They pick a President. Then they pick on him.

From the Humes File

If one is not paranoid when he enters the White House, he is when he leaves.

From the Humes File

Gresham's Law that "good money drives out bad" applies to the White House: flattery drives out truth.

From the Humes File

Listener—*Responsiveness*

When Calvin Coolidge was vice president, his successor as governor of Massachusetts, Channing Cox, paid him a visit. Cox asked how Coolidge had been able to see so many visitors a day when he was governor, yet always leave the office at 5:00 P.M., while Cox himself found he often left as late as 9:00 P.M. "Why the difference?" he asked. Coolidge replied, "YOU TALK BACK."

(And more of our politicians should do less talking and more listening . . .)

Opposition—*Narrow-mindedness*

One of the basic elements in British Prime Minister David Lloyd George's domestic policy was Home Rule. The prime minister considered that every one of the four countries of the United Kingdom should have local autonomy, subject only to the overriding authority of an Imperial Parliament. Lloyd George's "Federal Solution" was the subject of some heckling at one of his campaign stops. "Home Rule for Ireland! Home Rule for Wales! Home Rule for Scotland! Yes, and Home Rule for England, too," declaimed Lloyd George.

"Home Rule for Hell!" interrupted a heckler.

"QUITE RIGHT," said Lloyd George, "LET EVERY MAN SPEAK UP FOR HIS OWN COUNTRY."

(And the criticism from certain quarters would seem to indicate they seem to want hell or, at least, have no hope of salvation . . .)

Inactivity—*Silence*

Of all the presidents we have had, Calvin Coolidge may have had the least charisma. He was known for his silence. He had a very quiet five-plus years in the presidency; when he died in 1933 Dorothy Parker heard the news and she said, "HOW CAN THEY TELL?"

(Similarly, we haven't seen any sign of activity . . .)

Speech—*Brevity*

Coolidge's stinginess with words was even evident during his campaigns. At the time he was running for office, the most common method of reaching the people was the whistle-stop train. At one such stop, Coolidge stepped out to the rear of the railroad car and looked the crowd over. Then he calmly stepped back inside.

"What's the matter?" his campaign manager asked.

"THIS CROWD," Coolidge said, "IS TOO BIG FOR AN ANECDOTE AND TOO SMALL FOR AN ORATION."

(So let me just add one statement . . .)

Women—*Lobbies*

I sometimes think of what Franklin Roosevelt said when he was sworn into office for the third term and various representatives of the press were on hand to interview him. One reporter said, somewhat bluntly, "I suppose, Mr. President, that you will consult the powerful interests that control you in making new cabinet selections."

"YOUNG MAN," snapped F.D.R., "I WOULD ASK THAT YOU KEEP MY WIFE'S NAME OUT OF THIS."

(Well, I am not fool enough to believe that women can be kept out of any office . . .)

Misjudgment—*Criticism*

When President William Howard Taft was running for election, a heckler in Philadelphia threw a cabbage at him. Taft leaned down, picked it up and said, "I SEE THAT ONE OF MY HECKLERS HAS LOST HIS HEAD."

(And, at least figuratively, I think some of our opponents have lost their heads when they say . . .)

Taxes—*Government*

In the summer of 1941, President Roosevelt's son, Franklin Roosevelt, Jr., married the daughter of the Du Pont family in Delaware. At this unlikely alliance of the son of the head of the Democratic party and the daughter of one of the moguls of corporate capitalism, the gods must have been offended—for indeed the skies opened up.

A reporter at the wedding reception asked the President if the downpour dampened the spirit of the occasion. "No," replied Roosevelt, "IT IS ALWAYS A SPLENDID OCCASION WHEN I SEE SO MANY RICH GETTING SOAKED."

(Well, it is business that is being soaked today . . .)

Corporate Takeover—*Merger*

During World War I, Britain's foreign secretary visited Washington. On one afternoon his host was Franklin Delano Roosevelt, then the assistant secretary of the Navy. Roosevelt took the British Lord sightseeing to Mount Vernon.

While at Washington's home, Roosevelt pointed to the Potomac River and said, "Here is where George Washington supposedly threw a silver dollar across the river."

Replied Balfour, "I DON'T SEE WHY NOT. DIDN'T HE THROW A SOVEREIGN ACROSS THE ATLANTIC OCEAN."

(Like George Washington, our company resisted the threat of an overseas takeover.)

Vice President—*Respect*

During the three years Coolidge served as Harding's vice president, he had many reminders of the esteem accorded to people in his position. The Coolidges were staying in Washington at the Willard Hotel when a fire alarm went off in the middle of the night. Hundreds of guests, including the Vice President and Mrs. Coolidge, were herded into the lobby. Once Coolidge realized that it was a false alarm, he and his wife headed for the elevator.

"Just a minute," said the hotel's security chief. "Everyone stays in the lobby until we get the all-clear."

"I'm the Vice President," Coolidge said.

"Oh," the security chief said. "Sorry, Go right ahead."

Coolidge pressed the elevator button, but just then the

security chief had second thoughts. "Vice President?" he said. "Of what?"

"Of the United States," Coolidge answered.

"GET BACK OUT HERE," the security chief said. "I THOUGHT YOU WERE A VICE PRESIDENT OF THE HOTEL."

(Well, by the generous way you have been treating me, there is at least one vice-president who is getting respect.)

Clients—*Service Industry*

When Jimmy Carter was elected president in 1976, the press offered hundreds of stories about the new down-home style he would bring to the White House. During the period between Election Day and his Inauguration, Carter and his staff made preparations for the big move. One day, the president-elect and his wife asked the White House chef if they could expect the kind of meals they had always enjoyed.

"CERTAINLY," the chef said, "WE'VE BEEN FIXING THAT KIND OF FOOD FOR THE SERVANTS FOR YEARS."

(Well, the first thing the service industry has to know is their clients.)

Anniversary—*Happiness*

Shortly after Charles de Gaulle left the Presidency of France in 1968, Harold Macmillan, the ex–Prime Minister, invited the General and Madame de Gaulle to join Lady Macmillan and himself for dinner at the Georges V Hotel restaurant in Paris.

During the dinner, Macmillan turned to Madame de Gaulle and said, "Now that the General has retired, what gives you the greatest satisfaction?"

To his astonishment Madame de Gaulle replied *a penis*.

Macmillan was astonished to hear this from this old woman who was very pious and went everyday to Mass.

Then General de Gaulle interrupted. "HAROLD, YOU

HAVE MISUNDERSTOOD MADAME DE GAULLE'S FAULTY PRO-
NUNCIATION OF THE ENGLISH WORD 'HAPPINESS.'"

(However you spell or pronounce happiness, we wish you
years of it.)

Credibility—*Disbelief*

When Harry S. Truman was President, his daughter Margaret was a young woman who often received gentlemen
callers. Truman would greet each young swain and sometimes he would take him through the White House Rose
Garden. "You see the roses?" he would say. "The best damn
roses you've ever seen. You know why?"

The young gentleman would shake his head.

Truman would answer: "Manure. Cow manure—only
damn thing to make a great garden."

One night after a date, Margaret said to her mother,
"Don't you think we can get Father to say something besides
'manure.' Can't he say 'fertilizer?'"

"MARGARET," replied Mrs. Truman. "DO YOU KNOW HOW
LONG IT TOOK ME TO GET HIM TO SAY 'MANURE?'"

(Well, we don't need any fancy words to describe what
we have been hearing.)

Knowledge—*Expertise*

President Ulysses S. Grant boasted that he knew only two
tunes. "ONE OF THEM IS 'YANKEE DOODLE.' THE OTHER
ISN'T."

(Well, part of being an expert is knowing what you *don't*
know.)

Appreciation—*Staff*

At 330 pounds, William Howard Taft weighed more than
any other President. Before being elected President, Taft
was the governor-general of the Philippines. He sent his

reports to Elihu Root, secretary of war. At the end of one report, Taft wrote, "Took a long horseback ride today. Feel fine."

Root wired back, "HOW'S THE HORSE?"

(Similarly, I should ask how the staff survived considering the hard way they have been ridden . . .)

Substitute—*Executive*

When President Zachary Taylor died, Vice President Millard Fillmore became president.

On taking office, President Fillmore decided he should have a fancy carriage. He went with his assistant, Edward Moran, to look at a carriage. It was being sold by someone who was leaving Washington.

"It's very fine," said Fillmore. "But should a president be seen in a secondhand carriage?"

"REMEMBER, SIR," Moran reminded him, "THAT YOU'RE A SECONDHAND PRESIDENT."

(Well, today I am the acting chairman [or head] . . .)

Feminism—*Executive*

As an eminent politician, Britain's Prime Minister Margaret Thatcher had to deal with the usual brickbats about femininity being at odds with most forms of worldly success. As her husband, businessman Denis Thatcher found it helpful to exhibit a sense of humor when dealing with the nasty insinuations of the press. One reporter asked the tiresome question, "Who wears the pants in your family?"

"I DO," Denis Thatcher replied. Then, after a pause, he added, "I ALSO WASH AND IRON THEM."

Expense

John Kennedy's father was very, very rich. This led to rumors that he was going to give people money to vote for his son.

Making a joke of it, John Kennedy said, "I just got a letter from my father. He says, 'DON'T BUY ONE MORE VOTE THAN YOU NEED. I'M NOT GOING TO PAY FOR A LANDSLIDE.'"

Golf—*Purpose*

On a visit to Scotland, General Ulysses S. Grant was treated to a demonstration of a game he'd never heard of before—something called golf. His host wanted to show Grant how the game was played, even though he wasn't much of a golfer himself.

While Grant watched, the man placed a ball on a tee, stood back and took a swing. Although he missed the ball, he did tear up a patch of grass. He tried again, with the same result. Again and again he sent patches of dirt and grass into the air without once hitting the ball.

Grant looked from his perspiring host to the ball, then back to his host. "THERE SEEMS TO BE A FAIR AMOUNT OF EXERCISE IN THE GAME," he said, "BUT I FAIL TO SEE THE PURPOSE OF THE BALL."

(Well, I am asking what the purpose is of this new operation.)

Insincerity—*Posturing*

A delegation from Kansas, calling upon Theodore Roosevelt at Oyster Bay, was met by the President with coat and collar off. "I'm dee-lighted to see you," said the President, mopping his brow, "but I'm very busy putting in my hay now. Come down to the barn and we'll talk things over while I work." When they arrived at the barn there was no hay waiting to be thrown into the mow.

"James!" shouted the President to his hired man in the loft. "Where's that hay?"

"I'M SORRY, SIR," admitted James, poking his head out from the loft, "BUT I JUST AIN'T HAD THE TIME TO THROW IT

BACK SINCE YOU FORKED IT UP FOR YESTERDAY'S DELE-
GATION."

(And populist-posturing doesn't make a politician any
less high-handed or arbitrary . . .)

Options—*Choice*

Though there are a few options available, each one is fraught
with difficulty. In that sense I am like Chief Quannah
Parker. In his old age, after he quit the warpath, this famous
chief of the Comanches adopted many of the white man's
ways. But in one respect he clung to the custom of his
fathers. He continued to be a polygamist. Now the chief was
a friend and admirer of Theodore Roosevelt and on one
occasion when Roosevelt was touring Oklahoma he drove
out to Parker's camp to see him. With pride Parker pointed
out that he lived in a house like a white man, his children
went to a white man's school, and he himself dressed like a
white man.

So Roosevelt was moved to preach him a sermon on the
subject of morality. "See here, chief, why don't you set your
people a better example? A white man has only one wife—
he's allowed only one at a time. Here you are living with five
squaws. Why don't you give up four of them and remain
faithful to the fifth?"

Parker stood still a moment, considering the proposition.
Then he answered, "You are my great white father, and I will
do as you wish—on one condition."

"What is the condition?" asked Roosevelt.

"YOU PICK OUT THE ONE I AM TO LIVE WITH AND THEN
YOU GO KILL THE OTHER FOUR," answered Chief Parker.

(Well, let us look at the various options before us and see
why rejecting the other courses would cause difficulty.)

Copycat—*Imitation*

During the Coolidge administration, an overnight guest at the White House found himself in a hideously embarrassing predicament. At the family breakfast table he was seated at the President's right hand. To his surprise he saw Coolidge take his coffee cup, pour the greater portion of its contents into the deep saucer, and leisurely add a little bit of cream and a little sugar. The guest was so disconcerted that he lost his head. With a panicky feeling that it was incumbent upon him at the White House to do as the President did, he hastily decanted his own coffee into the saucer and followed suit. When he had accomplished this, he was frozen with horror to see the President take his own saucer and place it on the floor for the cat.

(Well, it is a danger to play "copycat" without thinking of the consequences . . .)

Misquote—*Out of Context*

As I look out in the audience, I see some of my friends in the Fourth Estate poised with pencil and notebook. I suppose I should do what Calvin Coolidge did in one of his rare press conferences. The first reporter asked him, "Do you have any comment about tariffs, Mr. President?"

"No," Coolidge replied.

The second reporter asked, "Do you have any comment about the farm bill?"

"No," Coolidge replied.

A third reporter asked, "Do you have any comment about the naval appropriation?"

"No," Coolidge replied.

As the reporters were leaving, Coolidge shouted to them, "AND DON'T QUOTE ME!"

(Well, I should have followed Silent Cal's advice . . .)

Politician—*Lawyer*

Our speaker today by his own admission is a politician. Now I know that that has become a pretty unrespectable word lately in the era of trillion dollar deficits. But we must remember that Lincoln, by his own admission, was also a politician—and proud of it. And so was Thomas Jefferson. I'd like to paraphrase the words of Pope Paul to former Prime Minister Golda Meir when she was in Rome visiting him. Being somewhat overwhelmed by the prospect of visiting the Pontiff of the Catholic Church, she said to a monsignor as she waited to go in for an audience, "Just think, Golda Meir, the daughter of a poor Milwaukee carpenter, going in to talk with the head of Rome."

"WATCH YOUR LANGUAGE," said the monsignor. "CARPENTRY IS CONSIDERED A VERY ESTEEMED PROFESSION AROUND HERE."

(Well, Lincoln was a politician as well as a lawyer and it proves both professions can invite respect on occasions.)

Competition—*Customer*

Sometimes leadership means the choice between two difficult alternatives. I remember President Johnson was once approached by his attorney general, Nicholas Katzenbach, on a delicate matter. "Mr. President," Katzenbach supposedly said, "I think the time has come for you to give public testimonial to J. Edgar Hoover's many years of service to his country as director of the Federal Bureau of Investigation and ask him to retire."

Johnson looked at Katzenbach and said, "Well, Nick, what if J. Edgar Hoover doesn't want to retire?"

"Mr. President," Katzenbach allegedly stated, "the time has come to bite the bullet and if necessary, request the resignation of the director."

"WELL," said L.B.J., "I'D JUST AS SOON HAVE J. EDGAR INSIDE THE TENT PISSING OUT THAN OUTSIDE THE TENT PISSING IN."

(And in the situation facing us, we'd rather keep that company as a customer than a competitor.)

Rhetoric—*Emptiness*

There is so much empty rhetoric spilling forth out of Washington these days—empty promises, empty statements of assurance. It reminds me of the time Senator Chauncey Depew was seated next to President William Howard Taft when the great after-dinner wit took note of Taft's obese girth. Looking at Taft's ample stomach, Senator Depew said, "I hope if it's a girl, Mr. President, that you will name it for your charming wife."

Then Taft stood and replied, "If it's a girl, I shall of course, Senator, name it for my lovely helpmate of many years. And if it's a boy, I shall claim the father's prerogative and name it William Howard Taft, Jr. BUT IF, AS I SUSPECT, IT IS ONLY A BAG OF WIND, I SHALL NAME IT CHAUNCEY DEPEW."

(Well, a lot of these promises we hear today are so much hot air . . .)

Conversion—*Recruit*

We are happy to gain any new recruits to our cause. We don't feel the way a certain Whig felt about the conversion of Andrew Jackson.

Andrew Jackson was as hated by Whigs as Franklin Delano Roosevelt was detested by Republicans during the New Deal days. One Whig, Tom Marshall of Nashville, described Jackson thus: "What a career has been that of Andrew Jackson! A career of success by brutal self-will. No impediment stood in his way. If he saw and fancied a pretty woman, even though she be another man's wife, he took possession of her. If he entered a horse race, he frightened or jockeyed his competitor. If he was opposed by an independent man, he crushed him. He saw the country prosperous under the Bank of the United States and shattered it from turret to foundation stone. His rule has been ruin to the people, his counsel full of calamity. AND NOW, WHEN HE IS APPROACHING HIS LAST HOURS, WHEN GOOD MEN ARE PRAYING THAT HE BE PUNISHED FOR HIS MISDEEDS, HE TURNS PRESBYTERIAN AND CHEATS THE DEVIL HIMSELF."

Departure—*Promotion*

When William McKinley was president, he wanted to nominate the eminent New York lawyer, Joseph Choate, to a diplomatic post. Knowing that the New York Republican boss, Tom Platt, despised Choate, McKinley asked Platt to discuss the matter with him in the White House.

"Platt," he said, "I'm thinking of sending Choate on a foreign mission to an embassy."

Platt replied, "MR. PRESIDENT, THE 'FOREIGNER' YOU SEND HIM, THE BETTER!"

(On the contrary, we are not happy that our honoree is leaving us soon . . .)

Candor—*Insincerity*

The nonagenarian Alice Longworth, the daughter of Theodore Roosevelt, was known in Washington for her caustic wit. Once she was asked her opinion of her distant cousin, Franklin Roosevelt. She answered, "I've always found Franklin a charming and delightful person to be with." Then she added, "ACTUALLY THERE ARE ONLY TWO THINGS I DISLIKE ABOUT FRANKLIN . . . HIS FACE."

(What we would like to see in Washington is less double-dealing and more straight talking about . . .)

Accomplishments—*Honoree*

In October 1963 the Earl of Home resigned his peerage and became head of the Conservative Party and prime minister. On his first day in the House of Commons, Harold Wilson, leader of the socialist party sarcastically asked him: "Why does being the 13th Earl of Home give you any special qualification to be prime minister?"

Home replied, "ACTUALLY, IT GIVES ME NO MORE QUALIFICATIONS THAN BEING THE THIRTEENTH MR. WILSON."

(Well, although our speaker does come from a distinguished family, it is his accomplishments that earned for him . . .)

Mess—*Problem*

At the Republican Convention in 1936, Alf Landon, the young Governor of Kansas, was nominated to run against President Roosevelt. For his running mate, he sounded out Styles Bridges, a fellow Republican governor from New Hampshire.

"No," Bridges replied. "CAN'T YOU JUST HEAR FRANKLIN ROOSEVELT SINGING ON THE RADIO, 'LANDON, BRIDGES FALLING DOWN, FALLING DOWN.'"

(Well, I don't mean to sound like Chicken Little, but something will be falling down . . .)

Mess—*Problem*

George Earl was governor of Pennsylvania during the Depression, when Franklin Roosevelt was president. They called Earl's administration in Harrisburg "the little New Deal" because of Earl's emulation of F.D.R. The Pennsylvanian's devotion to F.D.R. was only exceeded by his love of the opposite sex.

In the summer heat, the Governor would live at the com-

mand headquarters of the Pennsylvania National Guard
twenty miles outside Harrisburg. The wooded area also
served as a convenient trysting place for his amours. When
he wanted to set up a date with a woman he was involved
with, he would evade the State Police bodyguard detail by
excusing himself to go to the outhouse some forty yards
from the cabin and then hang his hat outside on the door to
signal his love interest that the coast was clear. She would
then leave her car to go to their special spot in the grove
nearby.

Unfortunately, once when Earl entered the privy to take
care of some pressing business first, the floor collapsed and
the chief executive of Pennsylvania fell into the 12-foot pit.
Not until nightfall did the State Police become worried
about the missing governor and rescue him.

IT IS ONE OF THE FIRST RECORDED CASES WHEN AN EXEC-
UTIVE FOUND HIMSELF, LITERALLY AS WELL AS FIGURATIVELY,
THAT HE WAS IN IT UP TO HIS NECK!

Vice President—*Vice*

It was Woodrow Wilson's vice president, Thomas Marshall,
who said, "What this country needs is a good 10-cent cigar."
Once Marshall asked the President if he could read his book
on government. Wilson kindly gave him a copy with the
inscription: "TO MY FAVORITE VICE."

(And, to my favorite vice president, whose vices are
few . . .)

Support—*Appreciation*

When Dwight David Eisenhower was President, one of his
most loyal supporters in the Senate was Thruston Morton. It
was said of Morton, who hailed from Kentucky, that he was
trying to singlehandedly consume one of his state's most
famous products.

One day a senator complained about Morton's drinking. This was a senator whose record of voting for the Eisenhower program was less than solid—even though the President had campaigned strongly for him.

Eisenhower drilled the man's face with two blue eyes and said, "ONE THING ABOUT THRUSTON, HE NEVER GETS SO DRUNK THAT HE DISREMEMBERS HIS FRIENDS!"

(Well, tonight we have with us one who has never *disremembered* his friends.)

Opportunity—*Advancement*

In 1928 President Coolidge issued his famous "I do not choose to run" statement. Afterwards, he was besieged by reporters asking for more details. One of the more persistent reporters followed Mr. Coolidge to the door of his library.

"Exactly why don't you want to be president again, Mr. Coolidge?"

The former president turned and looked the reporter squarely in the eye. "BECAUSE," he answered, "THERE'S NO CHANCE FOR ADVANCEMENT."

(Well, in our company there is great opportunity for advancement for those who have distinguished themselves with excellence, and today we want . . .)

Lukewarm—*Unenthusiastic*

My feelings are somewhat like those of President Grover Cleveland when his party nominated populist William Jennings Bryan to be the nominee. When asked if he would support Bryan, Cleveland answered: "I'M STILL A DEMOCRAT—BUT VERY STILL."

Disapproval—*Distance*

In 1844, the newly elected President Polk called on his mentor and fellow Tennessean Andrew Jackson. Polk informed the former President that he had asked James Buchanan to be his Secretary of State.

"Good Heavens," roared Old Hickory, "why in tarnation would you pick him?"

"Well, General, didn't you name him minister to Russia?"

"OF COURSE I DID. THAT WAS BECAUSE WE DIDN'T HAVE A MINISTRY TO THE SOUTH POLE. I WANTED HIM AND HIS IDEAS AS FAR AWAY FROM ME AS POSSIBLE."

(Well, let me distance myself from . . .)

Change—*Circumstances*

In 1958, Senate Majority Leader Lyndon Johnson was asked by a reporter what he thought of the speech Vice President Nixon had given before leaving for South America. Johnson drawled. "Pure chicken shit."

Weeks later, Nixon returned from his Latin America trip where he had heroically faced down Communist mob demonstrations. As his plane touched down in Washington, the first to greet him was Johnson. "Welcome home, Dick," he said.

Afterwards the same reporter said to Johnson, "Senator, a couple of weeks ago you likened Nixon and his policies to poultry excrement."

"SON," replied Lyndon, "YOU REPORTERS DON'T UNDERSTAND HOW OVERNIGHT CHICKEN SHIT CAN BECOME CHICKEN SALAD."

(Similarly, circumstances have radically changed since we . . .)

PARISH AND PULPIT

The pious ones at Plymouth reaching the Rock, first fell upon their knees and then upon the aborigines.

William Evart

He changed nothing for his preaching and it was worth it too.

Mark Twain

As the French say, there are three sexes—men, women and clergymen.

Sydney Smith

Luther was guilty of two crimes; he struck the Pope in his crown and the monks in their belly.

Erasmus

To all things clergic I am allergic.

Alexander Woolcott

God created man and then woman, but the atheist created himself.

From the Humes File

Truth—*Cheap*

A thrifty widow wanted the town's most famous minister to give a eulogy at her husband's services. The minister said, "For $200, I will deliver a eulogy that will enshrine your husband in the hearts of the entire city for the next ten years." "That's too much," said the widow. "I could give a pretty good talk for $100," said the minister reluctantly. "Nothing fancy, you understand, but no one will be able to doubt the solid virtues and endearing qualities of your late spouse." "That's still too much," said the widow. "Can't you give me anything for about $15?" "I SUPPOSE I CAN," admitted the minister, "BUT I MUST WARN YOU THAT FOR THAT PRICE I WILL HAVE TO TELL THE TRUTH ABOUT HIM."

(Well, we can't afford to tell anything less than the truth about . . .)

Leadership—*Direction*

At the synagogue the rabbi was delivering a sermon on leadership, using Moses as his example. One old gentleman in the back interrupted the sermon, stating, "Moses was a fink." The rabbi ignored the man and continued. A little later the old man yelled out again. "Moses was a schlemiel." The rabbi felt he had to stop. He asked, "Why do you profane the memory of our great leader?"

"WELL, FOR FORTY YEARS HE KEPT THE CHILDREN OF ISRAEL WANDERING IN THE DESERT AND THEN HE FINALLY BROUGHT THEM TO THE ONLY MIDDLE EASTERN COUNTRY WITHOUT OIL."

(Well, leadership is demanded today and leadership means direction . . .)

Introduction—*Familiarity*

We remember in the movie *The Hunchback of Notre Dame* that Quasimodo hired an assistant to help out with his bell-ringing chores. Quasimodo explained how to swing the bell clapper, then stressed how important it was to move out of the way before the clapper made its return.

The assistant was careless, however. He swung the clapper but failed to get out of the way in time. The clapper hit him in the face and he fell from the tower.

Quasimodo rushed to the street, where a crowd had already gathered. "Do you know this man?" they asked him.

"No," Quasimodo answered. "BUT HIS FACE RINGS A BELL."

(The accomplishments of our speaker tonight ring a bell with all of us . . .)

Cost—*Prohibitive*

At the revival tent meeting the evangelist preacher exhausted the faithful. At the end of his fiery sermon, he concluded, "All of those who want to go to heaven, raise their hands." One man in the back did not raise his hand, so the preacher asked him, "Don't you want to go to Heaven?"

"YES, BUT I DIDN'T THINK I HAD TO SIGN UP FOR THE BUS-LOAD TONIGHT!"

(Well, when we signed the deal, we did not anticipate the heavy costs . . .)

Contract—*Review*

An executive from the Budweiser Brewing Company called on the Pope. "Your Holiness, we would like to give one million dollars to the Vatican."

The Pope answered, "We bless you for your Christian charity."

"But we have just one request, the executive continued. We would like for you to substitute *beer* for *bread* in 'Give us our daily bread.'"

"This is an outrage, I demand . . . "

"Please, Your Holiness, we could give ten million dollars."

"You realize what you are asking? This is a sacrilege."

"We could give 100 million."

"I ask you to leave . . . immediately!"

As soon as the executive had gone, the Pope asked Father Giuseppe, the Vatican secretary of state, to come into his chambers. Then the Pope recounted to Father Giuseppe the details of his meeting with the beer company representative. Father Giuseppe shook his head in disbelief, saying, "It is a cardinal sin—a crime—by the laws of the Holy Church. It is simony."

"YES, I KNOW," replied the Pope. "BUT COULD YOU BRING ME FOR REVIEW THE CONTRACT WE HAVE WITH PEPPERIDGE FARM."

(Well, we are going to have to review our contract with . . .)

Women—*Expertise*

Back in the nineteenth century, Susan B. Anthony, the tireless fighter for women's rights, had a problem similar to Mrs. Thatcher's—a constant difficulty in being taken seriously by men. She was once confronted by William Phillips, a well-known abolitionist. "You are not married," Phillips said to her. "You have no business discussing marriage."

Holding her temper, Susan B. Anthony replied, "AND YOU ARE NOT A SLAVE, MR. PHILLIPS. SO WHAT BUSINESS DO YOU HAVE LECTURING ON SLAVERY?"

Familiarity—*Roots*

It's like old home week being here speaking to fellow Presbyterians. This is the faith of my fathers and it is where I got my religion. When I think of a church such as this, I think of a lady back in my hometown who was one of those Pentecostal types. She took a trip to England and went to church on Sunday morning at Westminster Abbey. There were the clergy in all their robes, with all the accompanying pomp and ceremony, and the woman didn't think she would hear anything that would remind her of her own revivalist heritage. But when the clergyman got up, after all the kneeling and standing and the liturgy, he began to preach from the Bible.

Well, that quite amazed the woman. The the clergyman said a few things she agreed with, and she was moved to call out, "Amen, brother!" This of course shook the congregation, and the minister almost lost his train of thought. He said something else she agreed with and she said, "Preach it, brother!"

Finally, an usher came and tapped her on the shoulder and said, "Madam, you can't do that in here."

"But," she said, "I have got religion."

"YES," he replied, "BUT YOU DIDN'T GET IT HERE."

(Well, I am proud to say that I did get my religion, schooling and values right here . . .)

Purpose—*Director*

It is important to have an objective and to know where you are going. I recall what my old Presbyterian minister said one time when he was quizzed by a Lutheran pastor about his theology. The Lutheran asked my minister: "Don't you believe in pre-destination."

"Well, yes, in a way."

"Don't you believe in foreordainment?"

"Well, yes, in a way."

"Well, I suppose if you knew that as a Presbyterian you were going to hell, you'd accept it?"

"I'D RATHER BE A PRESBYTERIAN KNOWING I AM GOING TO HELL THAN A LUTHERAN NOT KNOWING WHERE THE HELL I AM GOING."

(So today I want to start out by examining just where we are going . . .)

Tolerance—*Brotherhood*

As a protestant, I suppose I should feel out of place addressing a Catholic group. But I don't think it matters what church you go to, as long as you go—all churches do the work of the Lord. I recall the famous exchange between Billy Graham and Fulton Sheen. Coming out of a meeting they had just attended together, Graham offered the Monsignor a ride. After all, said Graham, "We both are engaged in God's work."

"YES," Monsignor Sheen replied, "YOU IN YOUR WAY, AND I IN HIS!"

(Well, I may be no theologian, but I know the type of work your organization does, and surely your work must be His work . . .)

Competition—*Rivalry*

The Pope called together a meeting of the cardinals and said, "I have some good news for you and some bad news. The good news is this. Our blessed Savior, the Lord Jesus Christ, has returned to earth for the long-awaited Second Coming, and the Day of Judgment is at hand."

There was an exalted silence for a few moments and then one cardinal said, "But Holy Father, with good news like that, what's the bad news?"

"THE BAD NEWS IS THAT THE INFORMATION REACHED US FROM SALT LAKE CITY."

(Well, we don't want to be hearing about the latest developments in our industry from the competition . . .)

Originality—*Plagiarism*

I can't claim that this idea is original with me. In fact, I feel somewhat like the minister I once knew who so thoroughly bored the members of his congregation that they asked him to leave. "Give me one more chance," he pleaded.

The congregation turned out in force the next Sunday and heard him deliver, to their surprise and delight, the most inspired sermon heard for years. After the service, everyone shook his hand warmly. One man, an elder of the church, said, "You must stay, with an increase in salary, of course."

The minister accepted. Then the elder said, "That was the greatest sermon I have ever heard. But tell me one thing. As you began to speak you raised two fingers of your left hand, and at the end you held up two fingers of your right hand. What was the significance of those gestures?"

"THOSE," answered the minister, "WERE THE QUOTATION MARKS."

Expertise—*Inexperience*

We have been hearing some beautiful rhetoric on the problem. But my reaction is not unlike that of the two ladies in Boston who heard the bishop give a rousing sermon on the beauties of married life. The ladies left the church feeling uplifted and contented. "'T'was a fine sermon His Reverence gave us this morning,'" observed one.

"THAT IT WAS," agreed the other, "AND I WISH I KNEW AS LITTLE ABOUT THE MATTER AS HE DOES."

(Well today we have with us someone with proven expertise and practical experience . . .)

Blame—*Responsibility*

In a town in County Kerry, Ireland, Father O'Reilly was known for his implacable hatred of the English. Every Sunday he laced his sermon with denunciations of "Perfidious Albion," the treacherous Sassenach who was the root cause of every problem in Ireland. The bile Father O'Reilly spewed was so venomous it came to the attention of his Bishop in Dublin. The Bishop called him in and told him that on pain of defrocking he was to desist in his denunciations of the English.

O'Reilly contritely nodded his assent. But the next Sunday, he gave a sermon on the Last Supper. Father O'Reilly told his parishioners, "And the Lord Jesus said, 'One of you will betray me.' And Judas Iscariot spoke up and cried out, 'BLIMEY—YOU CAN'T BELIEVE . . . I MEAN FOR 'EAVEN'S SIKE, GUV'NOR, YOU DON'T THINK IT'S ME?'"

(And when we cry out at the conditions we must look at ourselves and ask . . .)

[Note: If you can't put on a Cockney as well as Irish accent, don't tell this story. If you can, *this is a great story to tell Irish groups*.]

Minority—*Alone*

The preacher in a small town had become very perturbed, and he decided to lay it on the line to the congregation. "Brothers, sisters," he said solemnly, "it has come to my attention that there are tales to the effect that immorality is rampant in our fair town. To be specific, it is being said that there is not one virgin left here. This vile lie must and shall be refuted. In order to do so, I ask every virgin in the congregation to rise."

Not a woman stirred.

The preacher said, "I understand the modesty that would make a young lady hesitate to announce her condition publicly, but it is necessary to do so. Young women, I demand those to rise who are truly virgins."

And still not a woman stirred.

Wrath now moved the preacher. "Will you, for the fear of experiencing a small shame, incur a great one? This is an order from the Almighty: Let all virgins stand!"

And as his thunderous tones died away, a young lady, far in the rear, with a baby in her arms, rose bashfully. The preacher stared with astonishment at the baby, then said, "Young woman, I'm asking *virgins* to stand."

And the young lady answered indignantly, "WELL, DO YOU EXPECT THIS SIX-MONTH OLD GIRL TO STAND BY HERSELF?"

(Well, in this endeavor we are not alone.)

Market—*Change*

Mother Theresa called the Pope and said, "Your Holiness, I think I have concluded my work in India. I am at your service. What can I do to help God's children?"

The Pope replied, "Go to Ethiopia—the starvation and suffering there cries out for a ministering angel."

A month later Mother Theresa called the Pope again. "Your Holiness, I think God's work has been done. We've organized the food supply and every child is getting three meals a day. Where should I go next?"

"Thailand," he answered, "The refugee camps are horrendous with people pouring in from Laos and Cambodia."

A month later Mother Theresa called again. "Your Holiness, my work is finished. The camps have been organized; medical help found; disease wiped out. Where should I go next?"

"Hollywood, or rather, Beverly Hills," the Pope answered. "The unbridled lust, the sordid venality, the rampant materialism . . . all cry out for the spirit of God."

Months passed with no word. Finally, after four months, the Pope decided to call Mother Theresa in California. After six rings, a recorded message played: "HI THERE, BABE, THIS IS TERI. SAY YOUR PIECE AND I'LL BE BACK LATER. CIAO!"

(Well, we all know a move to a new market can change things entirely.)

Retirement—*Endurance*

On the occasion of my retirement I have some regrets but I don't feel like one of the novices who had taken a vow of silence in the enclosed convent. The rule was that they were allowed to speak two syllables per year to the Mother Superior, and that was all. After her first year, one novice had her session with the Superior. "Well, sister," asked the Superior, "what would you like to say? Remember, only two syllables."

"Beds hard," said the novice.

"But they're clean and good for the back, I think you'll find. I'm sorry you feel as you do. God bless you, sister."

At the end of the second year, the novice was again asked what she would like to say.

"Food sucks," she replied.

"But, sister," said the Superior, "it's made of the best whole-ground wheat, and the water is natural spring water, very good for the health. God bless you."

And so the third year came around, and this time the novice was carrying her possessions in a small sack. "Well, sister, what have you to say this year?"

"I QUIT."

(Well, I'm quitting too but I look back on my years with great satisfaction and fond memories.)

Mistakes—*Trends*

Some years ago there was an Archbishop of Canterbury who was an inveterate addict of crossword puzzles.

One morning when he was struggling with the puzzle in the morning paper, he turned to his young assistant, who was dean of the Cathedral.

"I say there, Dean, you were a First in English at Corpus Christi. What is a four-letter word for 'intercourse' ending with the letter 'k'?"

The Dean looked up from his account work and said, "Talk."

The Archbishop nodded, and then added, "COULD YOU LEND ME YOUR ERASER?"

(Similarly we leap to the wrong conclusion if we base our policy on insufficient evidence.)

PORTRAIT GALLERY

Art is either a plagiarist or revolutionist.

Paul Gauguin

Whenever I enjoy anything in art, it means it's mighty poor.

Mark Twain

There are only two styles of portrait painting—the serious and the smirk.

Charles Dickens

Let art alone. She's got anough guys sleeping with her.

From the Humes File

Activity—*Results*

Maxfield Parrish, the artist, was once lolling around in his studio passing the time with his model. All of a sudden he heard in the distance his wife, who knew of Parrish's disinclination for work. "QUICK!" he said to the model. "I HEAR MY WIFE COMING. TAKE OFF YOUR CLOTHES."

(Similarly, it is time for us to strip down for action.)

Bureaucracy—*Regulations*

Some of the new regulations we have to conform to remind me of the problem the famous art store Parke Bernet had in the 1960s. When they dedicated a new building in 1966, they commissioned Sir Charles Wheeler to sculpt a work for the entrance over the door. The result was an Aphrodite, entitled "Venus in Manhattan". The bare-bosomed goddess gave abundant evidence of her generous charms in beauty and love. The problem was that the size of the bosom protruded into city space—violating city ordinance. It was ordered to be torn down.

Fortunately, truce came to "the battle of bulge." After negotiating through their law firm, Parke Bernet agreed to pay twenty dollars a year. Actually, it was cheap considering that bosoms have often been rented for a lot more, but it does indicate the nitpicking effect of bureaucratic regulations.

Specialty—*Liabilities*

A certain eye specialist once successfully treated the great surrealist painter Salvador Dali. For his fee, the specialist requested that Dali paint something for him, on a subject of Dali's own choosing.

The grateful Dali therefore painted an enormous eye in meticulous detail and, in its very pupil, he placed a small but perfect portrait of the doctor.

The ophthalmologist looked at the painting with awe and astonishment and said, "WELL, SEÑOR DALI, I CAN ONLY SAY THAT I AM GLAD I AM NOT A PROCTOLOGIST."

(We all have an attractive side and one that is not as attractive. A different perspective paints a different picture. I am relieved that you have pictured me from the perspective of my strengths . . .)

Expert—*Second-Guess*

Pablo Picasso sat at an outdoor cafe in Paris, enjoying a drink with an American soldier. When Picasso explained the kind of art he was known for, the soldier shook his head.

"Sorry, but I don't like modern art," he said.

"Why not?" Picasso asked.

"Modern paintings aren't realistic," the soldier said. "I like paintings that look just like the things they're paintings of."

Picasso didn't react to this comment. Instead, he waited until the solder offered to show him some pictures of his girlfriend back home. Picasso took one of the pictures and looked at it for several seconds.

"MY GOODNESS," he said, "IS SHE REALLY THIS SMALL?"

(It is always risky for the amateur to second-guess the expert. Knowledge and experience offer a better perspective on things.)

PRESS GALLERY

News: the rough draft of history.

Ben Bradlee

Television is called a medium because it is neither rare nor well done.

Ernie Kovacs

The most truthful part of a newspaper are its advertisements.

Thomas Jefferson

The papers are not always reliable. That is to say they lie and *re-lie*.

Abraham Lincoln

I hope we never live to see the day when a thing is as bad as some of our newspapers make it.

Will Rogers

Journalism is in fact history on the run.

From the Humes File

Change—*Arrangements*

A young reporter happened to be in Johnstown, Pennsylvania, during the terrible flood of 1889. He started his dispatch thus: "God sat on a hill here last night and watched disaster and death sweep through this community."

His editor promptly wired back: "FORGET THE FLOOD—INTERVIEW GOD."

(Well, events have forced us to change our arrangements.)

Facts—*Coverup*

A president's dodging of the press is nothing new. It began back with George Washington and continued with everyone who succeeded him. For example, his immediate successor, John Adams, was repeatedly asked for an interview by a woman reporter named Mary Robinson. Adams' lack of response challenged her ingenuity.

Adams was the first president to live in what we now call the White House. The journalist decided to investigate Adams' habits. She learned that he regularly took an early dawn dip in the stream behind the White House. So one morning she appeared while the President was bathing. Grabbing his clothes in her hands, she shouted: "MR. PRESIDENT, NOW YOU HAVE TO ANSWER MY QUESTIONS!"

(John Adams could not cover up. He had to give the bare facts.)

Involvement—*Women*

Susan B. Anthony called on editor Horace Greeley one day in 1860 to ask for his newspaper's support for women's suffrage. Greeley was not sympathetic. He was an opponent of women's rights, mainly because he considered women to be of no military value. "What would you do," he asked, "in the event of a civil war?"

"I would do just what you would do," she replied. "I WOULD SIT IN MY OFFICE AND WRITE ARTICLES URGING OTHER PEOPLE TO GO AND FIGHT."

Honoree—*Humanity*

Churchill's son, Randolph, emulated his father by working in a journalism career. His daily columns were known for their vitriolic personal attacks on politicians whose opinions he opposed.

One day Randolph was rushed to the hospital with a spleen attack. The doctor removed his spleen, then ran tests and found there was no malignancy.

When Ian MacLeod, a sometime Conservative Party foe of Randolph's, heard the medical news, he remarked. "AMAZING THAT THEY FOUND THE ONE THING IN HIS BODY THAT WASN'T MALIGNANT."

(Well, tonight we honor someone who doesn't have a mean bone in his body.)

PUBLISHER'S ROW

Of the making of books there is no end.

Ecclesiastes

My library is dukedom large enough.

William Shakespeare

No one but a blockhead ever wrote except for money.

Samuel Johnson

A classic is something that everyone wants to have read but no one wants to read.

Mark Twain

Practically everyone in New York has half a mind to write a book—and does.

Groucho Marx

Writing a book is an adventure; it begins as an amusement, then it becomes a mistress, then a master, and, finally, a tyrant.

Winston Churchill

Some want a book to read—others just to read a book.

Winston Churchill

Many a novelist begins with a wealth of thought and ends with the thought of wealth.

From the Humes File

Writers are often paid by the word—never by the thought.

From the Humes File

Service Industry—*Clients*

William Faulkner, famous author of *Sanctuary* and other novels of the South, once served as postmaster at the University of Mississippi. When he decided to quit the job, he wrote a letter to the Postmaster General in Washington, which is still gleefully shown there to preferred visitors.

"As long as I live under the capitalist system," stated Faulkner, "I EXPECT TO HAVE MY LIFE INFLUENCED BY THE DEMANDS OF MONEYED PEOPLE. BUT I WILL BE DAMNED IF I PROPOSE TO BE AT THE BECK AND CALL OF EVERY ITINERANT SCOUNDREL WHO HAS THREE CENTS TO INVEST IN A POSTAGE STAMP. THIS, SIR, IS MY RESIGNATION."

(Well, those of us in the business of serving the public know the foundation . . .)

Outsider—*Hospitality*

Voltaire was highly regarded by many people in his own country, but to most people in England, he was just another Frenchman. When he visited London in 1727, he actually had good reason to fear for his life. Walking along a street one day, he found himself facing an angry crowd of people. Calls of "Hang the Frenchman!" came from the throng. Voltaire, however, was too quick to be outwitted by an unruly mob. Taking a couple of steps backward, he called out, "ENGLISHMEN! YOU WANT TO KILL ME BECAUSE I AM A FRENCHMAN? AM I NOT ALREADY PUNISHED ENOUGH IN NOT BEING AN ENGLISHMAN?"

The crowd not only applauded, they saw to it that Voltaire got home safely.

(I hope that as an outsider speaking on a controversial topic today, I get home safely too.)

Denial—*Retraction*

Alexander Solzhenitsyn was asked by a Western reporter how he existed as a writer in the Soviet Union.

"Splendidly," he answered. Then the Russian novelist added, "It's splendid as long as you follow a few basic rules:

First: don't think.

Second: if you think, don't talk.

Third: if you talk, don't write.

Fourth: if you write, don't publish.

Fifth: if you publish, don't sign your name and,

Last: if you sign, WRITE A DENIAL."

Change

One miserable, cold, rainy New Year's Day, the bartender at the Algonquin sighted Robert Benchley suddenly come from the wet street into the bar.

The breathless Benchley said, "I MUST GET OUT OF THESE WET CLOTHES AND INTO A DRY MARTINI."

Packaging—*Labeling*

Of course, so much depends on how we package this idea. It's like marketing a book these days, where more creativity seems to go into developing the title than the story. Publishers follows the Maugham rule, which comes from the time a young writer who had just completed his first work approached Somerset Maugham and asked, "Mr. Maugham, I've just written a novel but have been unable to come up with an intriguing title. Your books have such wonderful titles: *Cakes and Ale, Of Human Bondage, The Razor's Edge*. Could you help me with my title by reading the book?"

"There is no necessity for reading your book," replied Maugham. "Are there drums in it?"

"No, it's not that kind of story. You see, it deals with . . . "

Maugham then asked, "Are there any bugles in it?"

"No, certainly not," was the response. "No, you don't understand, it's about . . . "

"WELL THEN," replied the famous author, "CALL IT *No Drums, No Bugles*."

Capital—*Investment*

We would risk in this venture the cardinal sin. The author John Updike referred to this. He was visiting a small New England town to get background material for a novel. As he walked around talking with people, he noticed that there was one man whom everyone avoided as they passed him. The writer finally asked one of the citizens who the fellow was.

"Please don't ask," replied the citizen. "We just don't talk about him in town."

Even more puzzled, the writer went into the local news-paper office and asked the editor, "Who is this man? A mur-derer, a rapist, a thief, what?"

The editor grew tense and said in a low voice, "No, none of those. The town could live with that." Then he whispered, "BUT HE DIPPED INTO HIS CAPITAL!"

(Well, would we be risking our capital investment if we . . . ?)

Age—*Retirement*

When I contemplate old age, I remember what Somerset Maugham once said. Maugham had always been bothered by a hesitation or stutter in his speech. He was invited to address one of the most prestigious groups in England on his eightieth birthday. After dinner he rose, thanked his hosts, took a sip from his glass of water and began, "Old age has many benefits . . . "

There followed a long and painful pause, while he turned to the head table for help, sipped some more water, shuffled his notes and several times tried to speak. At last, holding the audience firmly in his grasp, he said, "I'M TRYING TO THINK OF SOME," and sat down.

(Well, contrary to Somerset Maugham I can think of some . . .)

Perspective—*Angle*

Perhaps we have been looking at this problem from only one side. The writer Robert Benchley, when he was a student at Harvard, took a course in international relations. Benchley, whose mind was agile but who didn't do much serious study-ing, came into the exam unprepared and was faced with this question: "Discuss the influence of the northern fisheries case upon international relations."

Benchley pondered a bit and then began his essay. "I SHALL DISCUSS THE NORTHERN FISHERIES CASE FROM THE POINT OF VIEW OF THE FISH."

(Well, perhaps we should look at the problem from another perspective.)

Involvement—*Inaction*

British playwright George Bernard Shaw once received an invitation from a celebrity hunter which read, "Lady X will be at home Thursday between four and six."

The author returned the card. Underneath the printed message, he had written: "MR. BERNARD SHAW LIKEWISE."

(Similarly, it would be wise to stay away from . . .)

Looks—*Honoree*

Isadora Duncan, the great dancer, once wrote to playwright George Bernard Shaw the suggestion, "We two ought to have a child, so it could inherit my beauty and your brains."

Shaw reportedly wrote back, "MADAM, I AM FLAT-TERED—BUT SUPPOSE IT TURNED OUT TO HAVE MY BEAUTY AND YOUR BRAINS?"

(Well, tonight we honor someone who has good looks as well as leadership ability . . .)

Conviction—*Sales*

The wife of Mark Twain was always chiding him on his profanity. One day, to shame her husband, she intoned a litany of unexpurgated Anglo-Saxon words at him.

"DEAR," Twain remarked, "YOU HAVE THE WORDS BUT NOT THE MUSIC."

(Similarly, I know that in your calls you know the right words, but is your heart in it?)

Neutrality—*Silence*

Late in his life, Mark Twain, at the urging of his wife, attended a lecture in Elmira, New York. Two theologians spoke on damnation and eternal punishment. As Elmira's most famous citizen, Twain was asked by the Chairwoman to comment after the preachers spoke.

"MADAM," replied Twain, "YOU MUST EXCUSE ME, I AM SILENT BECAUSE OF NECESSITY. I HAVE FRIENDS IN BOTH PLACES."

WALLS OF BUREAUCRACY

The people are fed-up with government. They think it doesn't work and they are right.

Richard Nixon

The perfect bureaucrat everywhere is the man who manages to make no decisions and escape all responsibility.

Brooke Atkinson

I think we do have more machinery of government than is necessary—too many parasites living on the labors of the industrious.

Thomas Jefferson

Government is like a baby—an alimentary canal with a big appetite at one end and no sense of responsibility at the other.

Ronald Reagan

Many a politician who's been appointed acts as if he's been annointed.

From the Humes File

Most governments would be better with fewer fact-finders and more fact-facers.

From the Humes File

Communication—*Corporatese*

During the early years of World War II, when the nation faced the threat of bombing on the east coast by Germany and the west coast by Japan, the General Services Administration designed a poster to be placed in the thousands of rooms in Federal Office Buildings. A G.S. 18 bureaucrat proudly read to President Roosevelt the words of the placard: "It is obligatory that all illumination be extinguished when the premises are vacated."

F.D.R.'s reaction: "DAMN IT, WHY CAN'T THEY SAY 'PUT OUT THE LIGHTS WHEN YOU LEAVE?'"

(Can we too, reduce to a few simple words what this report means?)

Failure—*Loss*

The only way I can describe such losses is as 'unrealized' profits or 'constructive' investment. I think of what a friend of my grandfather's once did when he had to fill out an application for an insurance policy. One of the questions he had to answer was, "How old was your father when he died, and of what did he die?"

The problem was that his father had been hanged, but he did not want to put that on his application. He puzzled over it for quite a while. Finally he wrote, "MY FATHER WAS SIXTY-FIVE WHEN HE DIED. HE CAME TO HIS END WHILE PARTICIPATING IN A PUBLIC FUNCTION WHEN THE PLATFORM GAVE WAY."

(I prefer to call a loss a loss. It is however, mitigated by the net profits . . .)

Communication—*Clarity*

Sometimes we executives are too fond of the polysyllabic *corporatese* or *bureaucratese*. It reminds me of the plumber who wrote to the Bureau of Standards, saying that he found hydrochloric acid excellent for cleaning drains. He inquired whether the Bureau thought it was okay. Their answer: "The efficiency of hydrochloric acid is indisputable, but the chlorine residue is incompatible with metallic permanence."

The plumber wrote back thanking the Bureau and expressing his pleasure that they agreed with him. The people at the Bureau were alarmed that they had been misunderstood, so they replied. "We cannot assume responsibility for the production of toxic and noxious residues with hydrochloric acid, and we suggest you use an alternative procedure."

The plumber wrote again, saying that he was glad they were keeping in touch, he was happy to know about their responsibilities, and that he was continuing to use HCL.

The Bureau sent a final communication, a telegram: "DON'T USE HCL . . . (STOP) . . . IT EATS HELL OUT OF THE PIPES."

(Well, sometimes you have to speak in a language everyone understands.)

Affirmative Action—*Women*

An Affirmative Action official of the State of Pennsylvania wrote to a business officer of a company whose policies were being investigated: "Please send to this office a list of all your employees broken down by sex."

Some time later, this reply was received: "AS FAR AS WE CAN TELL, NONE OF OUR EMPLOYEES IS BROKEN DOWN BY SEX."

(And while none of us is broken down by sex, we are sometimes worn down by filling in all those forms . . .)

Government—*Accountability*

We all get frustrated by governmental delays and half-assed ways of doing things. A friend of mine once had a stint at the Pentagon. Now he was a hard worker and he had a very nice, well-furnished office. However, he soon began to behave strangely. First, he shoved his desk out into the space also occupied by his secretary's desk. Then a few days later, as he was leaving for the day, he pushed his desk out into one of the many long corridors. He worked there for a few days and then he shoved his desk into the men's room and set up work there.

All of this had not escaped the notice of his fellow workers. It seemed more and more strange to them, so strange that they did not dare ask the officer himself what he was doing. Instead, they went to the division psychiatrist and asked him to ask the officer.

So the psychiatrist walked into the men's room, sat on the edge of the officer's desk and asked, "Why have you kept moving your desk? Especially, why into the men's room?"

"WELL," said the officer, "I FIGURE THAT THIS IS THE ONLY PLACE IN THE PENTAGON WHERE THEY KNOW WHAT THEY'RE DOING!"

Subject Index

Name Index